Earthquakes in London

Mike Bartlett's plays include *My Child* (Royal Court Theatre, 2007); *Artefacts* (Bush Theatre/Nabokov/59E59, 2008) which won the Old Vic New Voices Award; *Contractions* (Royal Court Theatre, 2008); *Cock* (Royal Court Theatre, 2009); *Earthquakes in London* (National Theatre/Headlong Theatre, 2010); and *Love, Love, Love* (Theatre Royal Plymouth/Paines Plough, 2010). Work for radio includes *Love Contract, The Family Man* (both BBC Radio 4, 2007); *Not Talking* (BBC Radio 3, 2006), which won the Writers' Guild Tinniswood Award and Society of Author's Imison Award; *The Steps, Liam* (both BBC Radio 4, 2009). He directed D.C. Moore's monologue *Honest* in its first production by the Royal & Derngate Theatre, Northampton, in 2010. He is currently Writer-in-Residence at the National Theatre and Associate Playwright at Paines Plough.

Mike Bartlett

Earthquakes in London

Bloomsbury Methuen Drama
An imprint of Bloomsbury Publishing Plc

B L O O M S B U R Y
LONDON • OXFORD • NEW YORK • NEW DELHI • SYDNEY

Bloomsbury Methuen Drama

An imprint of Bloomsbury Publishing Plc

Imprint previously known as Methuen Drama

50 Bedford Square	1385 Broadway
London	New York
WC1B 3DP	NY 10018
UK	USA

www.bloomsbury.com

Bloomsbury is a registered trade mark of Bloomsbury Publishing Plc

First published 2010
Reprinted with amendments to the text 2011
Reprinted 2012, 2014, 2015 (twice), 2016, 2017

British Library Cataloguing-in-Publication Data
A catalogue record for this book is available from the British Library.

ISBN: PB: 978-1-4081-3282-1
ePDF: 978-1-4081-3563-1
ePUB: 978-1-4081-3564-8

Library of Congress Cataloging-in-Publication Data
A catalog record for this book is available from the Library of Congress.

Series: Modern Plays

Typeset by MPS Limited, a Macmillan Company
Printed and bound in Great Britain

Earthquakes in London

This play could not have been written without Elyse Dodgson, Jonathan Donahoe, Clare Lizzimore, Rachel Wagstaff, Duncan Macmillan, the cast and production team, and particularly Miriam Buether, Rupert Goold and Ben Power.

The playscript that follows was correct at time of publication but might have changed during rehearsal.

Acknowledgements

'Deep Water' written by B. Gibbons/G. Barrow/A. Utley. Published by Chrysalis Music Ltd © 2008. Used by permission. All rights reserved.

'Rebellion (Lies)' words and music by Howard Bilerman, Win Butler, Régine Chassagne, Tim Kingsbury and Richard R. Parry © 2005, reproduced by permission of EMI Music Publishing Ltd, London W8 5SW.

Earthquakes in London was first performed in the Cottesloe Theatre at the National Theatre on 4 August 2010, in a co-production with Headlong Theatre. The cast was as follows:

Marina	Lucy May Barker
Tom	Gary Carr
Young Robert	Brian Ferguson
Grace / Receptionist / Jogger	Polly Frame
Simon / Roy	Tom Godwin
Colin	Tom Goodman-Hill
Carter	Michael Gould
Peter	Bryony Hannah
Businessman / Daniel / Student /	
Doctor Harris / Barman	Clive Hayward
Mrs Andrews	Anne Lacey
Supermarket Worker /	
Young Man / Tim	Syrus Lowe
Freya	Anna Madeley
Robert	Bill Paterson
Jasmine	Jessica Raine
Casey / Old Woman / Sally /	
Liberty	Maggie Service
Steve	Geoffrey Streatfeild
Sarah	Lia Williams

All other parts played by members of the Company.

This version of *Earthquakes in London* was first performed at Theatre Royal Plymouth on 22 September 2011, in a Headlong Theatre and National Theatre co-production. The cast was as follows:

Simon / Roy / WWII Officer /	
Polar Bear / Passer by 1	Ben Addis
Understudy / Dance Captain	Sam Archer
Peter / Mother	Helen Cripps
Tom	Kurt Egyiawan
Colin	Seán Gleeson

Marina / Mother / Understudy	Siubhan Harrison
Steve	John Hollingworth
Mrs Andrews	Maggie McCourt
Sarah	Tracy-Ann Oberman
Jasmine	Lucy Phelps
Supermarket Worker / Casey / Old Woman / Liberty / Mother	Nicola Sangster
Carter / Daniel / Police Officer / Dr Harris	Gyuri Sarossy
Robert	Paul Shelley
Grace / Receptionist / Mother / Jogger	Natalie Thomas
Young Robert / Business Man / Scammer / Bar Man / Dr Tim / Passer by 2	Joseph Thompson
Freya	Leah Whitaker

All other parts played by members of the Company.

Director Rupert Goold
Set Designer Miriam Buether
Costume Designer Katrina Lindsay
Lighting Designer Howard Harrison
Music Alex Baranowski
Projection Designer Jon Driscoll
Choreographer Scott Ambler
Sound Designer Gregory Clarke
Company Voice Work Jeannette Nelson

Project developed for Headlong by Ben Power

The creative team for the 2011 UK tour included:

Tour directed by Caroline Steinbeis
Associate Set Designer Lucy Sierra
Lighting Designer Tim Mitchell
Associate Projection Designer Emily Harding
Associate Projection Designer Paul Kenah
Associate Choreographer Steve Kirkham

Act One
Proper Coffee

Act Two
All The Mothers

Act Three
Mad Bitch

Act Four
Thomas Hood

Act Five
Certain Destruction

The play is presented using as much set, props and costume as possible. The stage should overflow with scenery, sound, backdrops, lighting, projection, etc. Everything is represented. It is too much. The play is about excess, and we should feel that.

Scenes crash into each other impolitely. They overflow, overlap. The production should always seem at risk of descending into chaos but never actually do so.

(/) means the next speech begins at that point
(–) means the next line interrupts
(. . .) at the end of a speech means it trails off. On its own it indicates a pressure, expectation or desire to speak.

A line with no full stop at the end indicates that the next speech follows on immediately.

A speech with no written dialogue indicates a character deliberately remaining silent.

Blank space between speeches in the dialogue indicates a silence equal to the length of the space.

Characters

Grace
Freya
Steve
Jasmine
Tom
Colin
Sarah
Simon
Supermarket Worker
Peter
Attendant
Businessman
Robert
Mrs Andrews
Many Students
Many Swimmers
Carter
Daniel
Roy
Young Man
Fifteen Mothers with pushchairs
Old Woman
Second World War Officer
Receptionist
Tim
Maryna
Liberty
Emily
Usher
Police Officer
Commuters
Passer by 1
Passer by 2
Other passers by
Doctor Harris
Nurse

Act One

1968

Cambridge.

Black and white.

Robert Crannock *is on a date with* **Grace**, *who is wearing a floral dress. They eat.* **Robert** *is awkward.*

'2525' is playing quietly in the background.

Robert	I'm sorry if the letter was too forward.
Grace	I liked the letter.
Robert	I got carried away, I'm sorry.
Grace	No.
Robert	I didn't mean to sound strange.
Grace	It wasn't strange. I liked it. Love letters in my pigeon-hole. Romantic.
	What do you do Robert? I mean I know you're a postgraduate, but what exactly do you ... do.
Robert	I'm doing a doctorate
Grace	In?
Robert	Atmospheric conditions on other planets.
Grace	Other planets? Like aliens?
Robert	Some of the work is to do with finding life yes.
Grace	Like Star Trek?
Robert	Well ... NASA are interested, so –
Grace	You're joking?

Robert	No.
Grace	NASA?
Robert	Yes.
Grace	Wow.
Robert	Yes.
Grace	Wow.
Robert	. . .
Grace	So how do you know? If there's life?
Robert	Well, all life gives off excretions of some kind. Gases, minerals.
Grace	We all give off gases?
Robert	Yes.
Grace	Even girls?
Robert	And all these gases –
Grace	Have you / researched this?
Robert	These excretions, from all of these creatures, they go up into the atmosphere, and you can imagine globally they would make quite a difference to its composition. So it follows that if we could accurately measure the composition of gases in the atmosphere of a planet like Mars, we could tell whether there was life.
Grace	And?
Robert	What?
Grace	Is there?
Robert	We don't know.
Grace	Oh.
Robert	We haven't done it yet. Not enough funding.

Grace	Right.
Robert	But as I say, NASA are interested.

She looks at him.

Grace	So all the time, every bit of life, animals, humans, everything, change the environment.
Robert	Yes. You are right now. The room is entirely different because you're in it.
Grace	You think?
Robert	Doesn't matter what I think. The atmosphere in this room is completely dependent on how much you move, whether you talk, if you've got a cold, how hot you are.
Grace	How hot I am?
Robert	Yes. Imagine if we all came in with a fever, the room would get much hotter, and then we'd get even hotter as a result, our fever would get worse and the room would become hotter in turn and so on and so on, upwards and upwards.
Grace	Hotter and hotter.
Robert	Exactly.
	Sorry. Whittering on. Supposed to be a date. I like your dress.
Grace	No, Robert, you've raised a very important question.
Robert	Really?
Grace	Yes. How hot do you think I am?
Robert	How hot?
Grace	How. Hot.

Robert   Well . . .

Oh.

You mean . . .

Grace   It's 1968. It's the summer. We're young. We can do what we want.

Robert *puts his hand on her forehead.*

She smiles.

Robert   Above average.

She smiles, and puts her hand on his head.

Grace   Boiling.

So what happens now?

They look at each other.

'2525' plays – gets louder. Cross fade scene and music into –

Proper Coffee

2010

A kettle boils.

Freya's *face isolated.* **Freya** *is singing along to a cover of '2525 Venice Beat' ft Tess Timony. She loves it.*

She sings some more.

We see **Freya**. *She is pregnant, wearing a man's shirt and making coffee in her kitchen. She has headphones on and dances. A television is on as well.*

Everything is done in rhythm – coffee, kettle ... sugar ... eats a spoonful herself.

We see **Steve** *in the shower. He hears her singing – bemused.*

Steve   Freya?

Freya *keeps on singing.*

Steve   Freya!

Freya *sings a bit more then takes a headphone out. The music is quieter.*

                   What?

Steve   What are you / singing?

Freya   I'm making coffee.

Steve   What?

Freya   Coffee! Do you want some?

Steve   Proper coffee?

Freya   It's always proper coffee.

Steve   What?

Freya   It's always proper coffee, / no one drinks *instant.*

Steve	What? I can't hear you! I'm in the shower! I can't hear you!

Freya *dances. The music becomes background in Starbucks.*
Tom *enters and offers a coffee to* **Jasmine.**

Tom	Full fat latte, two brown sugars, cream on top.
Jasmine	Do I know you?
Tom	Thought I'd do the honours. Did I get it right?
Jasmine	Don't know yet what does Rohypnol taste of?

She drinks a bit.

Tom	It was Marxist Criticism. We used to get our coffees at the same time. I liked the look of you, remembered your order. I'm Tom.
Jasmine	Yeah.
Tom	You're Jasmine. I heard you dropped out.
Jasmine	I had an argument with my lecturer.
Tom	What about?
Jasmine	Charles Dickens. Do you smoke?
Tom	I can.
Jasmine	Good boy.

Sarah *appears, talking to* **Simon,** *her assistant.*

Sarah	There aren't any plants.
Jasmine	Let's take this outside.
Sarah	Department of climate change, massive office and nothing's green. It's ridiculous.
Simon	It's on the list. And you need to put something in for Casey. She's leaving.

Sarah	Who's Casey?
Simon	By the wallchart? Under the window?
Sarah	Why's she going? Pregnant?
Simon	Redundant.
Sarah	Oh.
Simon	She's the chaff we talked about.
Sarah	Right. Yes. Right.
Simon	Smaller government. That's your policy.
Sarah	Not *my* policy Simon.
Simon	I'm afraid so, minister. What sort of plants do you want? You mean flowers?
Sarah	Here's ten for Casey. No not flowers. Flowers are dead. We want some life round here. Get a cheese plant. They still have those?

Freya *continues to make the coffee. Watches television at the same time.*

Colin *is in a supermarket and approaches a young assistant.*

Colin	Excuse me.
Sarah	They had them in the eighties.
Colin	I'm looking for a guava.
S. Worker	A what?
Colin	A guava.
S. Worker	What's that?
Colin	It's a vegetable.
S. Worker	Right.
Colin	Possibly a fruit.
S. Worker	Vegetables and shit are over there.

Colin   I'm sorry?

S. Worker   Vegetables and fruit and all that are over there.

Colin   I know but I've looked and I can't find it.

S. Worker   Probably don't have it then.

Colin   Probably.

S. Worker   Yeah.

Colin   Can you check?

S. Worker   Chhh.

Supermarket Worker *goes off to check. Still the music in the background.* **Jasmine** *and* **Tom** *are smoking outside.*

Jasmine   He's sat there opposite me, I said I'm not being funny but if you want two thousand words by Monday you can whistle, I have to *work* weekends, different for you *Gary*, fucking baby boomers, get your grant, got your degree then don't pay for your kids. So he says 'Do you have financial difficulties Jasmine?' and I'm like 'Gary. We all have financial difficulties, read the fucking papers'. Then he suddenly goes red, shouts that I'm 'thick as corrugated shit' whatever that means and says I only got in here because of who my sister is, so I lost it completely, threw a bookshelf at him.

Tom   A bookshelf?

Jasmine   It was *Bleak House* that got him in the eye, hardback so he had to go to hospital. They said I was a menace, attacking my lecturer with a weapon, I said something about the power of the written word and that was it. Out.

Tom   You don't look like a menace.

Jasmine   I am, Tom.

Supermarket Worker *comes back.*

S. Worker   Is this it?

Jasmine   I'm a natural fucking disaster.

Colin   How should I know? I don't know what a guava is. You tell me.

S. Worker   Yeah. This is it.

Colin   You're sure?

S. Worker   Yes.

Colin   Positive? Because this is important. I want you to understand that if I get home and this isn't a guava I'm in big trouble. So it follows that if I get home and this isn't a guava *you're* in big trouble, yes?

He reads her badge

                 ... Sue. You're in big trouble if this isn't a guava Sue. So.

                 You're sure?

S. Worker   Candice said it was and she's good with fruit.

Colin   Right, thanks.

Steve *enters with his suitcase, just as* **Freya**, *dancing, throws his coffee across the kitchen.* **Steve** *jumps out the way.* **Freya** *takes her headphones off.*

Freya   Didn't mean to do that. Oops.

Steve   Oops.

Steve *smiles and grabs a cloth instantly to mop it up.*

Freya   I can make another.

Steve   No, I have to go really, sorry ...

Freya	Don't be sorry.
Steve	Sorry I'm going at all.
Freya	Don't be – we need work, money, especially now, in the current climate, the way things are, that's what you say.
Steve	And it's only three days so –
Freya	Exactly. It's only three days so –
Steve	And you'll call me if anything –
Freya	Yes I'll call you if anything but nothing will nothing does nothing happens you know how it is round here these days.
Steve	I meant the baby.
Freya	Oh right the baby, well of course / the *baby*
Steve	You've got the number of / the hospital.
Freya	There was a programme on TV they're detecting something in the ground.
Steve	/ Freya?
Freya	They think something might – What? Yes I've got the number of the hospital. It's on the cupboard where you put it.
Steve	On the fridge.
Freya	On the fridge exactly. Are you sure you don't want any of this coffee? It's fair trade, kind of fruity, I like it.
Steve	I have to go – but you'll be alright?
Freya	The building might collapse while you're away.
Steve	Freya –
Freya	This is what I was trying to tell you. They said there's going to be an earthquake.

Steve   There's not.

Freya   There is.

Steve   Not here.

Freya   Right here, yes, they've detected tremors. It was on television. Do you fancy my sister?

Steve   What?

Freya   Not Sarah, obviously. Obviously not her. The other one. Jasmine.

Steve   No – Freya where does this / come from?

Freya   Why not? She's pretty.

Steve   She's nineteen.

Freya   Exactly. Thin, good-looking, bet she's good in bed. Of course you like her, you've had that thought. I used to look like that when we first met, I found some photographs, but what happened? Look at me now, fat and red like a massive blood clot or something. No wonder you don't want sex with me anymore. You should give her a call I'm serious I really am.

They look at each other. He moves closer, hugs her.

Steve   I don't think you're a massive blood clot.

Freya   Or something, I'm definitely something.

Steve   I wanted sex with you last night as it happens.

Freya   I can't I can't not with this, it's like it's watching.

Steve   I love you.

He kisses her tummy.

You too. I'll call when I get in.

Freya	I'm a bit lost at the moment, Steve, really. Don't go.

A moment.

Steve	Just three days. That's all. It's not as bad as you think. Never is.
Freya	Oh. Okay. Good.

He kisses her again and leaves. As the door shuts, **Freya** *jumps and the walls shake a little. She's scared. As* **Tom** *and* **Jasmine** *talk,* **Freya** *looks around her, then produces a packet of cigarettes and lights one.*

Tom	So your sister's famous?
Jasmine	My older sister is. Not in a good way. She's a politician. I didn't get in here because of my sister, I got in *despite* her, they *hate* her here.
Tom	What does she do?
Jasmine	When my mum died, my dad was a mess, so my sister looked after us but she was awful at it, really bad, because she's got absolutely no heart. Totally cold. She's made of metal, like the Terminator or something. But worse. She's like Terminator 3.

Sarah *is giving a speech for her team.*

Jasmine	Yeah, she's Terminator 3.
Sarah	Hello! Hi. We're so sorry to be seeing ... Casey ... go, leave. Yes. And although of course I absolutely believe our new ... policy of smaller government is the right one at this difficult time, it doesn't mean it's not a ... sadness ... when it impacts on someone personally. Casey's been fantastic as part of the ministerial team, a real laugh, ever since I've been here I've noticed that she's so ... *funny.* Anyway, Casey, we've had a whip round and got you this.

Sarah *gives a gift bag to* **Casey**. **Casey** *looks inside.*

Casey	A coffee machine.
Sarah	Yes.
Casey	I've been here five years.
Sarah	Well it's quite a good one I –
Casey	I don't drink coffee.
Sarah	You don't –
Casey	Herbal tea.
Sarah	Oh.
Casey	It's always been herbal tea.
Sarah	Right ... well ... someone hasn't done their research.
Casey	Research? Didn't anybody *know*? Jesus. You have no idea. We don't need *less government*. Everything's getting worse, and you're cutting the support. It's what the Tories would do crisis or not, but I voted Lib Dem. I voted for you. And what good did it do?

She looks around at everyone and gives the machine back.

> Put it on eBay. I'm leaving the country.

Sarah *steps down, speaks to her aide.*

Sarah	Good idea. Get the car.
Simon	You can't, you have a meeting in your office in three minutes.
Sarah	My stomach's rumbling.
Simon	Here. Egg salad. Tesco Express. You can eat it on the way back.

He gives her a horrible looking sandwich. She just stands for a moment. Exhausted. **Freya** *watches scenes from a documentary about the planet. Tectonics plates. Storms and hurricanes.*

> Are you ... ?

Another moment.

> Should I ...

She looks up and snaps out of it.

Sarah   What? Egg? Perfect.

Sarah *crams the sandwich into her mouth as she leaves.*

There's a knock on **Freya**'s *door, she goes to answer it.*

Tom *and* **Jasmine** *are going back inside.*

Jasmine   My sister's coming along tonight actually.

Tom   To what?

Jasmine   To what I do now. To my job. It's a bit
                  political too. You could come along if you
                  want. You'll be shocked. First time I've done
                  it. It's *very* political Tom. Very in-your-face
                  kind of political. You might not be able to
                  cope. It might be all too – *political* for you.
                  I've got a costume. So what do you think?
                  Want to risk it?

Tom *smiles.*

Tom   Yeah.

Freya *opens the door. It's* **Peter**, *a teenage boy with glasses in a grey
hoodie.*

Peter   Alright miss. You busy?

Freya   Peter. / What are you –

Peter   Is that whisky? You shouldn't be drinking if
                  you're pregnant, we saw it on a video in
                  Biology, Mr Greg showed it us yeah and it
                  said if you drink your baby ends up disabled
                  or something maybe it dies in you and they
                  have to pull it out with tweezers. Can I come

	in? I'm not doing very good. I want your advice.
Freya	How did you know where I live?
Peter	Went on the internet, put your name in, it's not difficult. Big bump you've got now. I need to talk. Can I come in?
Freya	I might get into trouble.
Peter	Nah you can't be a paedophile cos you're a woman and the hood's not cos I want to cut you it's cos it's raining, come on miss it's fucking biblical out here pardon my mouth used to talk didn't we? I liked it when we talked but you only come into school two days a week and not even that now. You're not busy clearly, you're watching TV. Is your husband in?
Freya	He's gone away.
Peter	His car's outside.
Freya	He got a taxi to the airport.
Peter	Yeah not supposed to fly any more though are you? How long's he gone for then?
Freya	Just a couple of days.
Peter	Bet you could do with the company then.
Freya	No.
Peter	Bet you could though.
Freya	Peter, you should go back to school.
Peter	No one visits you do they?
Freya	. . .
Peter	That's cos pregnant women are a bit of a pain. Sweaty and fat, stuck in the house, moaning and moaning, I don't think that

miss, but most people do that's why they don't visit. But I'm here.

I got you a flower.

He holds out a flower. She looks at him.

Freya   Thank you.

She takes the flower. He enters.

Sarah *is having a meeting with* **Carter** *in her office. She offers him a biscuit.*

Carter   Thank you. It's wonderful to meet you at last. Been a year. Thought I'd done something wrong.

Sarah   I've been very busy.

Carter   Well, better late than never. How are we doing?

Sarah   In two days time, after concluding my review, I recommend to the PM.

Carter   So I hear.

Sarah   And I thought you might want a heads up, to give you time to formulate a public response.

Carter   A heads up. Lovely. A response to what?

Sarah   We're nice people, Mr Carter.

Carter   I'm sure you are. Everyone's *nice* these days aren't they? Even me. I bought my son Adam a bike, for his birthday. Very expensive. He loved it. And what have you nice people got to offer us?

Sarah   I thought you might want to come on board with the decision now, rather than wasting time and effort fighting it.

Carter   The decision.

Sarah   Yes.

Another biscuit?

He looks at her.

Carter   Adam's learning quickly, he's six, he looked at his bike, and he said 'what's the bad news Dad?' He said you only buy me presents like this when there's bad news. He was right. His mother had run over the cat. This coalition government, whatever it is, you're supposed to be business friendly.

Sarah   We're very business / friendly, yes.

Carter   So what do you mean, what are we talking?

Sarah   The Heathrow decision played very well for us, the public didn't want that third runway, they were pleased we got in, and stopped it, so now I'll be recommending a complete halt to expansion.

Carter   Where?

Sarah   Everywhere.

Carter *is surprised.*

Carter   Look, Heathrow? Fine, I understand your position, you had to pull back, but it was assumed at the time, it was very strongly hoped, in fact, that in return, there would be balance.

Sarah   There isn't the need.

Carter   We let Heathrow go, but we get Birmingham, Edinburgh, London City instead – Belfast – that was understood.

Sarah   It can't be justified environmentally.

Carter   A few miles of concrete here and there, a couple of sheds, it's not the end of the world.

Have you talked to your colleagues, because I can't see this being very popular.

Sarah   A definitive halt to expansion will make a huge impact.

Carter   Only as a symbol.

Sarah   A symbol exactly. We have to be seen to be doing all we can to lower carbon emissions. We want to set an example.

Carter *looks at her.*

Carter   This is your big idea.

Sarah   If you like.

Carter   You're a symbol yourself really aren't you Sarah? Can I call you Sarah? Bet you never thought you'd be in power at all, but hung parliament, green credentials and a famous father –

Sarah   My position in this government has nothing to do with my father.

Carter   Everyone thinks it does.

Sarah   Then everyone is wrong.

Carter   Touched a nerve.

Sarah   Not at all.

Carter   You're upset.

Sarah   Do I look upset?

Carter   The way you rub your fingers together like that yes.

She's surprised for a second, but look back at him.

Sarah   We're not short of airports. In two days I have a meeting and I will put the case very firmly. The Prime Minister will make a

> decision, and that will be it. We'll announce next week.

Carter   You look tired.

Sarah   I work hard.

Carter   I don't think it's work.

Carter *takes a biscuit.*

> Before tomorrow, I'll change your mind.

Sarah   Really?

He passes the biscuits across.

Carter   Yes.

> Biscuit?

Freya *and* **Peter**.

Peter   I like your posters, you into Hitchcock?

Freya   They're my husband's.

Peter   And Grand Theft Auto. You play that a lot do you?

Freya   That's his too.

Peter   I find it a bit violent myself. I don't think driving round killing people should be in computer games. There's one where you can rape a girl. That's a bit weird they allow that considering everything that's gone on. Coldplay album? Everyone's got a Coldplay album these days, saw them on TV at Glastonbury they were rather good. What's yours then?

Freya   The books. I –

Peter   What are you reading at the moment?

Freya   Late Victorian poetry. Peter –

Peter	That sounds really incredibly boring. Can I sit down? / Are you going to give me a whisky? What's this?
Freya	Of course you can sit down. I don't know about a whisky –
Peter	Jees, you've been smoking as well, your baby's gonna be a scopoid by the time you're done. Fucking 'tato with what you're doing.
Freya	Peter, what do / you want?!
Peter	What's the programme?
Freya	They say there's going to be an earthquake.
Peter	Here?
Freya	My husband laughed as well but it's what they –
Peter	No they're right, it's true. There's going to be a massive tremor, the day after tomorrow, a huge seismic event, right in the capital. Things'll seem very different after that.

She looks at him. Shocked – how could he know?

	My problem is I don't have any friends. Atomisation. It's very common in society today. Increasingly people use internet dating to make a connection and find companionship but I'm only fourteen so I prefer porn. I am allowed a whisky actually. It is legal. In the home. If you're fourteen. So.
Freya	I'm not going to give you whisky.
Peter	I think you should though. Then we can talk properly.

She considers.

Freya	Why not?

Freya *goes to get* **Peter** *a drink.* **Peter** *sits down in the chair and relaxes as a* **Businessman** *on a plane, next to* **Steve**, *does the same.*

Businessman   Remember when you could smoke?

Steve   What?

Businessman   Smoke. On planes.

Steve   I see the ashtrays in the toilets. But I don't ever remember ...

Businessman   Fifteen years ago, you could go to the smoking section and smoke, didn't do any harm, no more planes went down, less than now, it was long before, you know ... *terrorism* – maybe it's linked. Frustrated Arabs. All they want is a fag. Cos they can't drink can they? Could be linked. Joking of course. You going to Scotland on business is it?

Steve   No.

Businessman   Holiday then?

Steve   It's personal.

Businessman   Oh right, well. Keep your own.

Fair enough.

Up to you.

Steve   I told my wife it's business.

Businessman   Oh.

Steve   But it isn't.

Businessman   Ah.

Yes.

Well.

I know all about that.

Steve   What?

Businesman   That.

Steve   No.

Businessman   Sometimes I'm in LA, and I always let her
                   know in advance, I say I won't, say it's not
                   good for me, but I drop a cheeky email, turn
                   up and we have the time of our lives. Keeps
                   my marriage healthy. Keeps me trim she
                   does. Carly.

Steve   Carly?

Businessman   Twenty-seven. Blonde. Tits. You know. Tits.
                   Twenty-seven. LA. Sun. Tits. Blonde. Jesus.
                   Says it all.

                   Why she goes for me I don't know, well I do,
                   flash the money a bit, but life's short isn't it so
                   you do what you have to, and my wife
                   knows, sure she's done the same, my view is,
                   if it keeps you trotting on, keeps you happy
                   and the kids don't know then what's the
                   harm? No you go for it mate. Full speed.

Steve   It's not ...

Businessman   Sorry?

Steve   It's not an affair.

Businessman   Oh. But you let me go on about ...

Steve   I didn't feel I could stop you.

Businessman   Always do this. Always end up talking to
                   strangers on planes. Must be nervous I
                   suppose.

Steve   You fly a lot?

Businessman   It's bad for you.

Steve   Bad for you?

Businessman Of course, the more you fly, the greater chance you'll be in a crash. It's not natural.

If God had meant us to fly, he'd have his own airline.

Rumbling. Turbulence or possibly the sound of thunder.

The lights flash.

'There She Goes My Beautiful World' By Nick Cave and The Bad Seeds

Jasmine *comes on dressed in branches and leaves.*

She holds a sign which says 'The willful destruction of the rainforest'

She dances.

She slowly peels off leaves and branches.

Eventually she is left with leaves in the vital places, à la Adam and Eve.

She picks up a sign

'Originally, there were six million square miles of tropical rainforest'

Another sign

'Only a third is left'

She raises her eyebrows.

She peels the leaves off her breasts.

There are cheers from the crowd.

Flirty eyes.

She picks up another sign.

It says 'Don't leave the world naked'

As she goes, leaves fall from the ceiling.

Freya *brings* **Peter** *his whisky then lights a cigarette.*

Peter Hmm. I'm enjoying this. This is good, really good whisky. Did you buy it?

Freya	Peter, if there's going to be an earthquake why aren't people scared?
Peter	I was in an earthquake once in Tokyo. Me and my parents were doing karaoke in this room –
Freya	Can you answer / my question please.
Peter	– and the floor started moving and the walls tilted, shook a bit but not like you imagine, everything just went ... drunk. Do you ever feel like that miss, stuck in this flat like you are, that the walls are moving and everything's becoming dangerous?
Freya	All the time.

Freya *drinks the whisky.*

But what can I do?

Tom *and* **Jasmine** *are in a bar.*

Tom	Never seen a stripper before.
Jasmine	It wasn't stripping.
Tom	This is a strip club.
Jasmine	It's burlesque.
Tom	You got your tits out.
Jasmine	You get your tits out in both yeah but in burlesque they're not the focus.
Tom	They were definitely the focus.
Jasmine	Well they're not supposed to be.
Tom	There's a man waving.

Colin *appears and waves. He's still carrying a carrier bag with the shopping.*

Jasmine	It's my sister's husband.

Tom	You invited your sister's husband?
Jasmine	I invited my sister. She said she'd come so I got *political*, thought she'd like it, but she texted at the last minute, said Colin was coming instead. Colin's been around since I was a kid, he was a banker, lost his job, now he's got time on his hands. Warning: He can be a bit –
Colin	Brought my shopping!
Jasmine	I can see that.
Colin	Bit weird. Well done!
Jasmine	You liked it?
Colin	You can really dance.
Jasmine	Yeah.
Colin	Haven't seen you perform since school.
Tom	And hasn't she grown?
Colin	Well ... I ... I suppose so.
Jasmine	This is Tom.
Colin	Oh right. Hello. Are you her latest ...
Tom	Latest?
Jasmine	Thanks Colin.
Tom	Her *latest*?
Colin	Squeeze.
Jasmine	Oh God.
Tom	We've only just met.
Colin	Well the night's young.
Jasmine	For fuck's sake.

An awkward pause.

Colin	I thought you made a very good point actually Jasmine.
Tom	There was a *point*?
Jasmine	The signs?
Tom	I wasn't really looking at the signs.
Colin	The destruction of the rainforest.
Tom	So that's why you were dressed as a bush.
Jasmine	A tree.
Tom	Certainly looked like a bush from where I was sitting.

Awkward.

Colin	Do you want a drink either of you?
Jasmine	No thanks Colin.
Tom	Nah.
Colin	Right.
	Well. Great to … see you. Jasmine.
	I should probably be going … got some milk … needs the fridge, asap, don't want it to …
	Smell, but really …
	Well done.
	Good work!
Jasmine	Good to see you.
Colin	Right.
	Bye.

A pause. He goes.

Jasmine	God.
Tom	Actually I did read the signs.

Jasmine	Really.
Tom	Yeah, I'm quite into the environment. My family from before, they're Eritrean? and they –
Jasmine	Er sorry to interrupt you but I've had enough of the environment, hear about it all the fucking time, I only did it for my sister and she didn't even turn up. I'll do a Nazi one next week probably. They love Nazis. Have you got any pills? You look like the sort of person that carries drugs around in their pocket.
Tom	A sort of black person you mean?
Jasmine	A sort of careless person I mean, who leaves their coat lying around.

She holds them up.

Found them earlier.

She opens the bag.

Shall I be mother?

Freya *and* **Peter**.

Peter	I'm spinning.
Freya	I know what you mean. I don't see anyone for days, the walls start shaking, so I think about going out but it's all shouting and dirt, so I stay in, but then ... I've started singing, ever since I got back. When I sing I forget she's there.
Peter	Got back from where? Can I have a cigarette?
Freya	I don't know what to do.
Peter	I didn't see anyone for three days once and got really paranoid my head was too big for

my body, but it's not, is it? Is it? Is it? Cos earlier Gary Franks said I looked weird, chased me out of school said I was special needs.

Freya   You are special needs.

Peter   Not in a bad way, not like those deaf kids you spend your time with.

Freya   Don't say that.

Peter   I can do an impression of a deaf person.

Freya   No.

Peter   I can, look, it's funny.

Freya   Don't.

Peter *moves closer to* **Freya** *– threatening.*

Peter   If you don't give me a cigarette I'll do an impression of a deaf person.

Freya   No!

                 Don't

                 Here.

She throws him the cigarettes, **Peter** *grabs them and stops. A throbbing beat has begun.* **Freya***'s in pain.*

Peter   I know cigarettes are supposed to be bad for you but apparently if you give up within five years you're pretty much back to normal and I'm very young so I think I'll be fine miss.

Freya   In my head.

Peter   Do you think that's right?

                 Miss?

                 Do you think I'm right about that?

                 Miss?

                 Miss?!

The sound of a plane in the distance.

A computer screen is projected.

Someone is writing.

Writing   'I feel that I would be right for the position of senior accounts manager as I am both strong ...

He deletes.

strong both as a team player and a leader.

Lights up on **Colin**, *who is typing.*

' ... I have demonstrated this on many occasions, leading my team through many years of excellent service over the last ten years. Ten. Years ...'

The cursor goes to Google.

It types.

Student

Girls

Party

Pictures.

As images appear the stage becomes full of students dancing in mini-skirts, boys with their tops off, grinding up against each other. Dance music gets slowly louder. In the middle are **Jasmine** *and* **Tom**. **Colin** *stands up, watching, wanting to be involved.*

Freya *is now faced away from* **Peter**, *leaning against a wall, a throbbing beat in her head.*

Peter *is trying to light the cigarette.*

Peter   As you know, I don't really like being outside, around lots of other people, but do you remember what you said miss? I'd stabbed Luke Reynolds with a compass, and

> got detention, and you said I couldn't just sit around feeling sorry for myself, I had to get off my arse and fucking do something. Find the good things.

Freya   I don't think I used those words.

Peter   You did use those words. You definitely said fucking do something. I found the honesty quite bracing. You're one of the only people in my life who tells me the truth.

Freya   So you think I should get up and –

Peter   I don't know, but what with the shaking

Freya   I was imagining it, the walls can't –

Peter   I didn't mean the walls.

Freya   Oh.

Peter   Your hands miss. Look.

Her hand is shaking.

> You should pack a bag and get out and see what's going on. Find the good things. Before it's too late.

They look at each other. He lights the cigarette, smiles and relaxes. **Freya** *leaves. Determined.*

Colin *watches them dancing. Enjoys it. He then changes the track on iTunes to Coldplay – 'Viva La Vida'. The students cheer – enjoying the cheese.*

Sarah *enters.*

Sarah   What's this?

Colin   Coldplay

Sarah   You bought a Coldplay album?

Colin   In Tesco on the way home yeah.

Sarah   That's the sort of thing boring middle-aged
                   women do.

Colin   Right.

Sarah   You don't look like a boring middle-aged
                   woman.

Colin   You do.

Sarah's *tired of the bickering.*

Sarah   Found anything yet?

Sarah *goes into the kitchen where the shopping is laid out.* **Colin**,
very quietly sings at the computer.

Colin *shouts through to the kitchen.*

Colin   You see this is the problem, that's always the
                   first thing you ask, you get in and you don't
                   kiss me, touch me, even look at me –

Sarah   What's this?

Sarah *is standing in the doorway holding a fruit.*

Colin   A guava.

Sarah   No.

Colin   Right.

Sarah   Get the ingredients. That's all I asked. It's
                   not a guava Colin, it's a plum. Find a job.
                   That's the problem. Not me. Find a fucking
                   job. I'll make a sandwich.

Sarah *goes.* **Colin** *keeps on singing to himself, restrained and shy,*
watching the students dance.

Steve *appears, trying to hide from the wind, and starts knocking on*
a door. **Tom** *dances with* **Jasmine**, *they kiss passionately.* **Colin**
watches. **Sarah** *makes a sandwich.* **Peter** *goes to the CDs and looks*
at them.

Sarah *goes to bed. The door is opened by* **Mrs Andrews**.

Mrs Andrews   Yes?

Steve   I'm here to see Mr Crannock.

Mrs Andrews   Mr Crannock is in bed.

Steve   I'm Steve Sullivan.
His daughter's husband?

Mrs Andrews *sighs.*

Mrs Andrews   Is he expecting you?

Steve   No.

Mrs Andrews   . . .

Steve   Please. It's very cold.

She lets him in. **Jasmine** *and* **Tom** *dance.* **Peter** *chooses a CD and puts it on – the same Coldplay song. Listens. Mouths along. He likes it.*

At the next chorus **Peter** *sings loudly like a choirboy.* **Colin** *still very quietly.*

Freya *appears with a bag, hat and coat, ready to go out.*

Freya   You can put the heating on if you like. The switch is in the hall,

Peter   What are you doing?

Freya   There's food in the fridge.

Peter   I didn't mean you should go now. It's raining cats and dogs out there, and you're pregnant, you probably shouldn't even stand up for too long, it might fall out or something.

Freya   You can stay here. You won't steal anything will you?

Peter   Can I watch your DVD's?

Freya   Yes.

Peter	Even the eighteens?
Freya	If you want.
Peter	Can I drink your whisky and vodka?
Freya	Whatever you like. You've got the place to yourself for a couple of days. Okay?
Peter	Okay.
Freya	Right.
	Okay ...
Peter	Are you going to be alright miss?
Freya	She's kicking. Stop it!
	The good things.
	I can't stay here.

Freya *opens the door and leaves.*

Peter *stands up and sings.*

The students join in, singing the backing vocals.

Peter *sings, the students dance, and* **Colin** *sits by his computer motionless and sad.*

Everyone sings as **Freya** *walks off into the night.*

Lights fade.

Music in the dark.

Music fades.

End of Act One.

Act Two

1973

Technicolour

Robert *and two businessmen,* **Daniel** *and* **Roy**. **Roy** *is smoking.*

Roy	Good to see you. Have a seat.
Robert	Thanks.
Roy	How's the baby?
Robert	Oh, you – ?
Roy	Daniel mentioned there was a baby. A baby girl.
Robert	Right, yes.
Daniel	Wonderful.
Roy	Wonderful. And your wife?
Robert	Very happy obviously, well we both are.
Roy	Very happy. You both are.
Daniel	Perfect.
Roy	Perfect. So. Robert. You're wondering why you're here? When does the main UK airline call in a Cambridge boffin like you? Well, our bods predict that in thirty years time they'll be thousands of planes in the sky, flying people all over the place, which makes us happy of course, because there's a lot of money to be made.
Robert	Yes.
Roy	But there are increasing concerns.
Daniel	Questions.
Roy	Sorry?

Daniel	Questions, I think Roy.
Roy	Questions, exactly, about what the effect will be of all this air travel? With the emissions. Into the atmosphere.
Robert	Right.
Roy	People are starting to get worried.
Daniel	Curious.
Roy	People are starting to become *curious* about what burning all that fuel might do. To the world.
Daniel	The environment.
Roy	The *environment*. So we thought we'd get an expert in who could do a study.
	Look into your crystal ball and tell us what's going to happen. So what do you think? Is it possible?
Robert	Well. We'd ... we'd need to model the world on a scale no one's done before. And ... well ... I don't want to be rude, but obviously you're hoping for a negative answer here aren't you?
Daniel	No no.
Roy	A what?
Daniel	He means do we want him to get us the result which says these fumes are doing no harm at all? Should he fix it?
Roy	Ah. No. Robert, you do your science and you tell us what you find.
	We won't interfere at all.
Robert	No interference.
Daniel	None.

Robert   Right.

Roy   And this is only the first phase. If this project seems promising, we're authorised to commission further work, over the next ten years.

Robert   Really?

Roy   Absolutely. Because your results might not just be useful for us, but many similar organisations. The motor industry, oil companies. They would all be very interested in promising results.

Robert   What do you mean promising?

Roy   Results that seem to be useful.

Daniel   Meaningful.

Roy   Right. *Meaningful.* I need a coffee.

Robert   Well I'm sure it's possible to achieve a certain clarity, but this is a very new subject, there's no real way of knowing how quantifiable in real terms the . . .

Roy   This would be the fee.

Robert   Right.

He reads it.

                  That's . . . Oh. Yes. That's good. I'm sure we could make a start with that.

Roy   No. Robert.

                  That's not the budget.

                  The project will have a separate budget.

                  That's your fee.

                  That's for you. To keep.

Daniel	And remember there's potential for a good deal more of this to come. I would imagine someone like you, in your position, academic, young family. This could make a real difference.
Robert	Yes.
Roy	Why don't you take it away and have a good old think?

All The Mothers

The present.

Hampstead Heath – Early morning. Birdsong.

Freya *is sat by the pond.*

A number of male swimmers are in the ponds, swimming. They have similar swimming hats and swimming costumes. One by one they come and stand in the fresh morning air. Birds fly past, a clear blue sky.

Freya *watches them for a while.*

One of the swimmers starts to play ukulele.

Freya *starts singing along to 'Deep Water' by Portishead. The first swimmer is surprised, but interested. Three other swimmers stand in a line and act as backing singers.*

Freya   *I'm drifting in deep waters*
                     Alone with my self-doubting again
                     I try not to struggle this time
                     For I will weather the storm

Sarah *gets to her desk, piled with papers. It's first thing, but she's exhausted – she sits down and makes a start.*

Jasmine *sits on the end of the bed, waits, upset.*

                     I gotta remember
                     (Gotta remember)
                     Don't fight it
                     (Don't fight it)
                     Even if I
                     (Even if I
                     Don't like it
                     (Don't like it)
                     Somehow turn me around
                     (Somehow turn me around)

                     No matter how far I drift
                     Deep waters
                     (Deep waters)
                     Won't scare me tonight

Sarah *picks up the phone.* **Freya**'s *phone rings. The swimmers look annoyed with* **Freya**.

Tom *appears, and* **Jasmine** *goes off with him.*

The swimmers go off.

She answers.

Sarah	I missed your call.
Freya	I thought we could meet up?
Sarah	I can hear birds.
Freya	I'm on the heath.
Sarah	Hampstead Heath?
Freya	Yeah, by the ponds. I packed a bag, left early.
Sarah	You don't live anywhere near Hampstead Heath.
Freya	Very early. Apparently there's a view where you can see the whole city.
Sarah	Parliament Hill.
Freya	I think I'm looking for that. So are we going to meet then?
Sarah	I could do Thursday?
Freya	I meant today really.
Sarah	I'm busy Freya.
Freya	You're always busy Freya, but Steve's not here and I couldn't get hold of Jasmine, / so I thought we could –
Sarah	Don't ask Jasmine, you called Jasmine?
Freya	You have got time, I know you have.

A beautiful perfect woman dressed in black with black sunglasses, pushing a pram goes past.

Sarah   Get here, to the department, for one o clock. We'll have twenty minutes. Well, ten. Come to the desk and tell them who you are.

Freya   Thanks.

Sarah   Right.

Sarah *hangs up. The mother accidentally drops a leaflet from the pram.* **Freya** *picks it up and reads it.*

Freya   A picnic, on Parliament Hill.

                   Perfect.

                   Excuse me.

Freya *follows the woman, off through the Heath*

Mr Crannock's *House.*

Steve *is asleep on the sofa.* **Mrs Andrews** *clatters in, open the curtains.*

Mrs Andrews   Are you not awake yet?

Steve *wakes up.*

                   How did you sleep?

Steve   How do you think?

Steve *stands up in just his boxer shorts, woozy.*

                   The sofa's too short, so I tried the floor, but there was a draught.

Mrs Andrews   Mr Sullivan ...

Steve   What?

Mrs Andrews   You're not at your best.

Steve   Oh.

He puts his jeans on. Then a t-shirt.

                   Isn't there a spare room?

Mrs Andrews   There's my room.

Steve	I'm sorry?
Mrs Andrews	If you'd called ahead, we could've made arrangements.
Steve	What do you mean?
Mrs Andrews	When your wife visited, I stayed at my sister's.
Steve	Oh – you ... Freya called ahead?
Mrs Andrews	Do you two not talk about these things? Now, Mr Crannock has got up and gone out. He starts very early, and won't be disturbed. You've never met I understand?
Steve	No.
Mrs Andrews	No, well if he trusts you you'll get a drink, if he likes you, he'll talk all night. He'll be back to the house later this afternoon, as will I.
Steve	What am I supposed to do until then? You've got no television, I didn't bring my computer, there's no reception on my phone.
Mrs Andrews	You'll have to occupy yourself I suppose.
Steve	With what?

Mrs Andrews *looks at him.*

Mrs Andrews	There's a radio.

Mrs Andrews *goes.*

Freya *sees an* **Old Woman** *laying flowers at a war memorial. The* **Old Woman** *wears a coat and headscarf.*

Freya	Excuse me.
Old Woman	Alright dear?
Freya	I like your flowers.

Old Woman   Thank you dear.

*The **Old Woman** smiles. They both look at the memorial.*

Was it . . . your husband?

Old Woman   Dunkirk.

Freya   And you still miss him?

Old Woman   I miss what went with him. How it was, when we were together.

Freya   Did you have children?

Old Woman   It was a different country then. England was made of wood and metal. Not plastic, like this. You know what I'm saying?

Freya   No I –

Old Woman   It had teacakes, cricket whites, cut grass. Yes? Blitz spirit, rooms full of smoke.

Freya   Okay. Yeah I suppose it / must've been

Old Woman   Short trousers, dinner jackets, tea dances.

Freya   I always wanted to go to a –

Old Woman   Devonshire cream, Coventry steel, the home guard, the muffin man, the post man, larders in the kitchen, fires in the living room, the damp smell of gravel in outdoor toilets. You don't know what I'm talking about.

Freya   No.

Old Woman   That was our England. All gone now of course. Things move so fast. The cars, the internet. Yes we had children, but I never see them. Always got something better to do.

So instead, I come to the heath.

And wait.

Freya   What for?

Old Woman   The silver lining. Soon it'll all be over.

They look at the memorial.

Simon *enters* **Sarah**'s *office.*

Simon   Your sister's at the front desk.

Sarah   Now?

Simon   Now.

Sarah   I said one o'clock.

Simon *hands* **Sarah** *an envelope.*

                   What's this?

Simon   Not sure. It just arrived. What about your sister?

Sarah   Send her up, and get me a Starbucks.

Simon   Skinny?

Sarah   No. Fat. Really fucking ... fat.

Simon *goes.* **Freya** *is with the* **Old Woman**

Freya   I'm looking I'm really looking for something good, happening now, but you're saying things are only getting worse.

Old Woman   Religious intolerance, economic collapse, tsunamis, riots ... it's the perfect conditions.

Freya   I don't understand.

Old Woman   Is it a boy?

Freya   A girl.

Old Woman   A little girl. Well. I hope she can fight.

A young man in a Second World War uniform comes on. He takes the **Old Woman**'s *arm and kisses her.*

Freya	What?
Old Woman	There's a gathering storm

He takes off her headscarf and she stands upright – a young couple from the 1940s.

Freya	How do you know?
Old Woman	Old people can predict the weather …

The man opens an umbrella and it starts to rain.

	You see?
Freya	She can fight. I've felt her kicking.
Old Woman	Haven't you got anyone to take you home?
Freya	No. He's …
	Gone.

*The **Old Woman** goes with her husband, just as a mother comes past with her pram. **Freya** goes off after her.*

Jasmine *enters **Sarah**'s office with **Tom**.*

Jasmine	I've got a problem.
Sarah	Where's Freya?
Jasmine	Where she normally is, probably – at home, eating crisps.
Sarah	Who's this?
Jasmine	He's the problem.
Sarah	Does he have a name?
Jasmine	Tom.

Sarah *takes them in for a second.*

Sarah	Okay. I'm going to look over my letters but I am listening.
Jasmine	Last night, I was at a party.

Sarah	Thought you were dancing last night.
Jasmine	After that. It was a porn star party, we all dressed as porn stars you know
Sarah	Not really.
Jasmine	And I went back with Tom. We fucked and stuff, and he was taking pictures on his phone I thought for fun yeah?
Sarah	Yep.
Jasmine	And then today this morning when I'm a bit morning-ey, just woken up, he tells me that his family in Africa are being affected by climate change and that you aren't doing anything so his family are going to die. Apparently you're making this big statement about 'airport expansion'.
Sarah	Next week, that's right.
Jasmine	So he says why don't we go and see your sister and get a commitment.
Sarah	And you said.
Jasmine	There's no way I could change her mind she doesn't listen to a word I say.
Sarah	Absolutely right.
Jasmine	But then he said he's only gone with me, he's only done any of it, so that he could blackmail you. He's part of some group or whatever. He says if he doesn't get an assurance, he'll send the pictures to the paper.
Sarah	What were they of?
Jasmine	The pictures? Drinking, puking. Us in his room fucking.

Sarah   Nothing illegal?

Jasmine   Nothing in the pictures.

Sarah   Does he speak?

Tom   This is happening, right now, to people like me, to my family. And if you don't believe me . . .

He gets papers out of his bag.

               Letters, photographs, measurements. Rainfall, crop growth, all from my family in Eritrea. Now, I realise you probably don't even know where Eritrea is but –

Sarah   Borders in the west, in the south, and in the southeast . . .

Tom   Yeah okay, yeah, exactly, and they're struggling to –

Sarah   The population's an estimated five million? The capital is – I assume you're going to tell me about the current and tangible effects of climate change on the agriculture, on the villages, your family.

Tom   You're aware of all that.

Sarah   That's sort of my job.

Tom   Then it's worse. You know what's going on and you still allow runways and flight paths. You don't listen, we've raised petitions, spoken to our MPs, all you say is you 'appreciate our view', you 'encourage the debate' – but nothing happens.

Sarah   You don't know what we're going to announce.

Tom   I can guess.

| Sarah | You can guess absolutely you can have a wild stab in the dark but you don't *know*. |

I want you to understand a couple of things Tom. Firstly my sister's a student. She has sex. So what? You think the public are going to be interested? *I'm* not interested.

Secondly, in this country you elect your government, and then we consult and make decisions based on what is right for the people. We take into account different factors – environmental, economic, social. It's complicated because we have to consider everything. Transport means investment. Investment means greater employment. Greater employment means less poverty, which presumably you're in favour of? That's why you have people like me, to make a *judgement*. So what are you doing, Tom? Blackmail? Of a democratically elected member of parliament?

Tom *slams his papers on her desk.*

Tom   It's a protest.

Sarah   Good. There. You've protested. It's over. Now delete the photos, get out of my office, stop wasting my time.

Tom   Are you going to read all this?

Sarah   I'm certainly going to file it.

Tom   You can't dismiss me.

Sarah   This isn't the student union Tom. We're the fucking government. Go away.

Tom *turns to go.* **Jasmine** *turns as well.*

Not you.

Tom *stares at* **Sarah** *for a moment. Then goes.*

Jasmine	I only came here for your sake.
Sarah	You didn't want your arse in the Daily Mail.
Jasmine	Wouldn't be the first time.
Sarah	What?
Jasmine	When I run out of toilet paper the Daily Mail's just what I need.
Sarah	You have absolutely no idea how hard I'm working, do you? How many meetings I have, the paperwork –
Jasmine	Yeah, Colin said you're always here.
Sarah	It's public office Jasmine. It's the most important thing in my life, I can't –
Jasmine	He'll leave you.
Sarah	What?
Jasmine	Colin. Surprised he hasn't already.
Sarah	
Jasmine	
Sarah	You have no idea.
Jasmine	I know what men want. And I bet you're not giving it to him. Fucking ice woman, frosty the snowbitch think you're all big and clever power tights and shoulder pads, fucking Thatcher look at you. I'd have been better off with Dad probably.
Sarah	Be careful Jasmine.
Jasmine	He can't have been worse than you.
Sarah	You've never met him.
Jasmine	You've never let me.

Sarah	Let you? You're nineteen. He's a shit Jasmine, if you don't believe me, yes please give him a call instead. Or you could talk to some friends about all your problems – you never do that either do you? For some reason you never have friends to turn to. You ever wonder why you're always being fucked over like this?
Jasmine	I'm not being –
Sarah	Again and again I think you are, clearly you are, you ever thought why?
Jasmine	You're jealous.
Sarah	Jasmine, when you want to know, just ask. I've got a whole thing ready to go, I know exactly what your problem is.
Jasmine	. . .
Sarah	You want to hear it?

Jasmine *is upset.* **Simon** *enters, interrupting.*

| **Simon** | One fat coffee. |

Jasmine *goes.* **Simon** *gives the coffee to* **Sarah***, as* **Sarah** *makes a phone call.*

Sarah	Call John Carter. Tell him I got the letter, and I want to meet, this afternoon.
Simon	You don't have time.
Sarah	I'll make time.

Simon *goes.* **Freya** *is on Parliament Hill looking for mothers. She answers the call.*

Freya	Do you know where Parliament Hill is?
Sarah	I'm sorry?
Freya	There's this big event, this afternoon. Why don't you come here?

Sarah	Freya –
Freya	A picnic. There's stalls, and a band. The sun's out. I'm going to buy some sandwiches. Ice cream.
Sarah	Can you listen. I've had to move things around, I can't meet you anymore.
Freya	You said you'd make time.
Sarah	I know but things change and you're alright aren't you? Your ... picnic.

A **Young Man***, dirty and sweaty, runs up to* **Freya** *grabs her arm.*

Young Man	Please! Please. Please. Please.
Sarah	Everything's just gone a bit mad here.
Young Man	My kid. My kid's in trouble.
Freya	Yeah, everything's gone a bit mad here too.
Sarah	Got to go.

She hangs up.

Young Man	He's in hospital, I've just found out, I need the bus fare to get down the road, I don't have any ... change ... I'm sorry, I'm really in a hurry. Shit. Shit.
Freya	How old is he?
Young Man	What?
Freya	Your kid.
Young Man	Seven. He fell over at school I think, I –
Freya	And you dropped everything and ran.
Young Man	Yeah –

She reaches in her pocket – pulls out the fiver.

Freya	It's all I've got. I was going to get lunch.
	Here.

She gives it to him.

Young Man   Bless you love. Bless you.

The **Young Man** *runs off, ecstatic.*

Freya   Good luck!

The sky gets darker.

Freya *feels a sharp kick.*

Freya   Ow!

Clutches her stomach.

Jasmine *is in the street, unhappy, in the rain.* **Tom** *is following her.*

Jasmine   It was basically rape.

Tom   What?

Jasmine   What you did. Bit like rape or something.

Tom   No it wasn't, you had a good time. I didn't plan it like –

Jasmine   So you took the pictures because –

Tom   You took the pictures. You suggested it. I was just hoping to persuade you to talk to your sister, but then when you wouldn't and I had the pictures on my phone –

Jasmine   No / no no

Tom   I realised I could do something.

Jasmine   Have you ever even been there?

Tom   What?

Jasmine   To ... You know.

Tom   Eritrea.

Jasmine   Yeah. You ever actually been there?

Tom   I want to but I'd have to fly so –

Jasmine	Right so, your family? Shut up. Never met them. Are you sorry? What you did to me?
Tom	I tried three times to talk you about it instead, but you just shouted me down, get another drink, walk away. So no I'm not sorry, you didn't leave me a choice.

She pushes him away and storms off, leaving him in the street.

Mrs Andrews *is sorting through table cloths.* **Steve** *talks to her. The clock strikes four o'clock.*

Steve	How much longer is he going to be?
Mrs Andrews	He'll be home soon.
Steve	I could help if you like? With that?
Mrs Andrews	Go and stand over there.

Steve *does as he's told.*

Steve	You were here when my wife visited.
Mrs Andrews	In the day, yes.
Steve	What was she like?
Mrs Andrews	I don't know. She was polite, she was like a young lady. I hope you know better than me.

Beat.

Steve	They talked.
Mrs Andrews	All night I believe.
Steve	What about?
Mrs Andrews	You think I was in there listening? I stayed at my sister's.

A pause.

Steve	You know he hasn't seen his children in years.

Mrs Andrews	Aye.
Steve	You know why?
Mrs Andrews	I stay out of his business. You'd best talk to him. If you're sensible, and you might be, you might not be, I don't know, but if you are, you'll not cross him.
Steve	Why not?

Mrs Andrews *takes a towel and begins unfolding it.*

Mrs Andrews	Because, Mr Sullivan, while I'll admit you don't look stupid, whilst I'll concede you seem to have some kind of brain, you're no genius.
Steve	And he is?
Mrs Andrews	Yes.
Steve	A genius?
Mrs Andrews	Aye.
Steve	What does that even mean?

The door bursts open and **Robert Crannock** *enters. A seventy-year-old man, in a raincoat, and holding a small wind turbine.*

| **Robert** | A person of extraordinary intellect and talent. |
| | A person who has great influence over another. Take this. |

He gives the turbine to **Steve**.

| | A wise man. A shaman. A prophet. |

Mrs Andrews *shuts the door and gives him the towel on cue.*

Mrs Andrews	Mr Crannock.
Steve	I'm sorry to just –
Robert	Shh. I've had the data, had that for a while, but now you're here in person, now I'm

| | looking at you ... you don't work too hard, that's clear, a sense of humour but nothing with edge. You used to be a sportsman. Cricket? |

Steve   Football.

Robert   Football. Ha! But that's been dropped. Your shirt's a bit tight round the sides, you've put on weight recently. You like things to be simple. Fish fingers and chips. Don't like posh food. You're that sort of man. Yes? Chicken nuggets and pizza. Ketchup. Beans. Children's food. You haven't cut your fingernails properly, tells me you're self-employed. Yes? Good.

So? Me?

Come on *Steve*. Who am I? Am I what you expected?

Steve   You're lonely. But I knew that already.

Robert   Oooh. Killer. But no actually, not so lonely. Mrs Andrews keeps me company. She's a blessing. Problem is. She loves me.

Mrs Andrews

Robert   Those *eyes*. I tell her, Mrs Andrews, it's not you, it's your *age*. It's prohibitive. I know why you're here.

Steve   Good.

Robert   And I'm not interested, could've told you over the phone. Now this ...

Robert *pours himself a drink.*

Is a very fine single malt. Should I be drinking at my age, at this time in the afternoon, you're thinking? You're not a whiskey drinker are you Steve?

Steve	Not really.
Robert	Not really? You are or you're not. Where did you sleep?
Steve	On the sofa.
Robert	We don't have a spare bed do we?
Mrs Andrews	No.
Robert	Flirting! Look at her. There isn't a bed, there you have it, straight from the horse's mouth – no offence Mrs A – and you didn't call ahead, so it looks like you're on the sofa again tonight.
Steve	If we can just talk now I can get going, I don't –
Robert	I work hard, you can see this I work all day I've got things to do. I'm very busy.
Steve	I've come all the way here –
Robert	So make the most of it there's hotels – scenery. A loch nearby, a castle.
Steve	I'm here because of Freya.
Robert	I know Steve, *I know* why you're here.
Steve	She said this about you.
Robert	What?
Steve	That you get angry quickly.
Robert	She told me about you too.
Steve	Did she?
Robert	About the problems.
Steve	What problems?
Robert	Exactly.
	Have you made up your mind?

Steve   What about?

Robert   Are you a drinker of whiskey?

Steve   Alright.

Robert   You are?

Steve   Yeah, I'll have one.

Robert   Good.

Steve

Robert   Good boy. Better.

                   Doing better.

He pours one. Gives it to **Steve**.

                   There.

They drink.

Steve   It's good.

Robert   Mine is. You've got the cheap stuff.

It is late and overcast now. Dark. Windy.

Jasmine *arrives at a bar. A* **Barman** *comes over.*

Jasmine   I want the strongest drink.

Barman   I'm sorry?

Jasmine   The most alcoholic drink you sell.

Barman   Look, it's only five.

Jasmine   Are you a clock?

Barman   What?

Jasmine   Cos you look like a barman, you work in a
                   bar, but you're telling me the time. It's quite
                   simple, I want to get as drunk as I can, as
                   quickly as possible, so –

Barman   Absinthe.

Jasmine   Two please.

Barman   One for you and one for ...

Jasmine   The sheer hell of it. Come on ...

She reads his name badge.

> Paul.
> Paul! This is urgent.
> I need to get off my face ...

Jasmine *hits the bar suddenly.*

> Come on!

The **Barman** *pours* **Jasmine** *her shots.* **Freya** *follows the two mothers to a picnic, listening to 'Happiness' by Goldfrapp. The sky is clouding over, getting darker.*

Meanwhile, **Carter** *is waiting in the street.* **Sarah** *approaches him, windswept, and unhappy.*

Sarah   I'm late I know. Long day. Where are we going?

Carter   Don't you have an umbrella?

Sarah   Clearly not.

Carter   This way.

They go off, under his umbrella.

The group of mothers in black with black prams and sunglasses appear again. They dance and sing, holding their wrapped up babies, showing them to each other, drinking their coffee and ignoring **Freya**.

They sing and dance to 'Happiness' by Goldfrapp.

Freya *watches them, and tries to take part.*

After a while **Freya** *takes a headphone out and speaks to them.*

Freya   Excuse me?

Mothers   Yes?

Freya   I'm here for the picnic.

The **Mothers** *look her up and down. Smile in a fake way.*

Mothers	Not being funny but –
Freya	Okay.
Mothers	Yeah.
Freya	My baby's kicking.
Mothers	How sweet!
Freya	Not in a good way.
Mothers	Ahhhh.
Freya	Do you worry about the future?
Mothers	Not really.
Freya	What might happen?
Mothers	No.
Freya	What might happen to your children?
Mothers	Henry's very bright, he's already reading. He'll go into hedge funds Or a surgeon. Something like that.
Freya	How was the birth?
Mothers	Natural.
Freya	How do you manage with it all?
Mothers	Easily.
Freya	None of you got down about it? None of you felt your child was a . . .
Mothers	A?
Freya	A mistake?
Mothers	No. God. No.
Freya	And what about people who are poorer than you?

Mothers   We do what we can.

Freya   Yes but –

Mothers   Charity work. Every Thursday. Primrose Hill. We carbon offset holidays.

You know.

Freya   But that's not enough, and if it's not enough, then what's the point.

Aaaahhh!

She clutches her belly again. They look at her for a moment, more serious now, almost threatening. They stand, wielding their children, almost like weapons.

Freya (*over singing*) Call me an ambulance.

Please.

Please!

The singing continues.

Then they slowly encircle her.
She is scared but has nowhere to go.

The women throw the babies up in the air.
They explode into black powder, like soot or dust, that covers everyone, and is blown about by the wind.

The music continues as the women disappear, **Freya** *falls to the floor, and the lights fade.*

End of Act Two.

Act Three

1973

Roy, Daniel *and* **Robert**.

Roy *and* **Daniel** *are looking through a few sheets of paper.* **Roy** *is smoking.*

Robert	It's just a preliminary document. To give you some idea of the way it's going.
Roy	We understand what it is.
Robert	So you know where it's headed. I thought it would be good to get your ... views.
	At this stage.
Roy	You think this is what will be in the final report.
Robert	The way it's going yes.
Roy	You can't imagine that they'll be any ... surprises.
Daniel	New factors.
Roy	New factors yes, still to come.
Robert	I can't see how there would be no.
Roy	Right. Can't see how there would be.
Daniel	Hmm.
Roy	Because the thing is, these aren't really the results we were expecting.
Daniel	They're not meaningful.
Roy	Meaningful.
	Exactly.
	What do they tell us?

Robert	Quite a lot actually. If you do this sort of work it's clear that releasing huge quantities of carbon dioxide into the atmosphere at such a high altitude will cause heat to be reflected rather than released, potentially causing rising temperatures and –
Roy	No. Robert. Hang on. With respect. All that you've just said, that tells you a lot. It tells *us* very little. We wondered if there was any way you could make them *meaningful* to us.
Robert	
Roy	If there was a way the report could focus on something that we can understand. Because if there was. A clearer *focus*. This could be the start of a very fruitful relationship.
Robert	Yes but this is –
Roy	As we spoke about.
Robert	Right.
Roy	Perhaps it's a question of how you present it. Perhaps it's as simple as that?
Robert	
Daniel	Or maybe you need some more resources. To see things clearly. Is that what we're talking about? Are we talking about resources? Or should we discuss the fee?
Robert	It's not about money . . .

Daniel   Of course.

Daniel *writes on a piece of paper.*

He passes it across. **Robert** *reads it.*

> I think you should keep going. There's six months before the final report. That's a long time. Anything could happen.

Mad Bitch

The evening. Dark.

Freya *is at the reception of a hospital. She meets* **Maryna**, *a Polish cleaner, who is playing 'I Am Not A Robot' on a tinny radio.*

Freya	You have to help me.
Maryna	Nie potrafie mowie po angielsku (I don't understand English).
Freya	It's hurting. It's really – Ow!

A **Receptionist** *comes over.*

Maryna	Jestem tulko sprazatacza, / idz ee znajdz lekarza (I'm just the cleaner, go / and talk to a doctor.)
Freya	This is a hospital you have / to help me.
Receptionist	Alright ...
Maryna	She says it hurts.
Receptionist	I can see that.

Maryna *looks* **Freya** *in the eyes.*

Maryna	Po burzy zawsze slonce przychodzi (After the storm, the sun always comes).
Receptionist	Thank you Maryna, I'll deal with it.

Maryna *picks up her mop and watches.*

	Now what's your name?
Freya	I'm not telling you my name.
Receptionist	You can't be treated until we / have some information –
Freya	I'm pregnant. You have to treat me.
Receptionist	Let's just start with a / name, can you give me a

Freya   I pay my taxes, the whole point is you treat
                   me so treat me I don't want to talk to you,
                   where's the doctor?

Receptionist   You will see a doctor, I'm just trying to get
                   some details. How / long have you been –

Freya   I'm not telling you anything, I don't like you,
                   I'm in pain. It's kicking so hard. Ow!

Receptionist   How many weeks?

Freya

Receptionist   How many weeks?

Freya   Let me in!

Dr Tim *comes in.*

Dr Tim   Is there a problem?

Maryna   I think you should let her in.

Jasmine *is knocking on* **Colin**'s *front door.*

Colin   Alright!

As the receptionist takes **Freya** *into the hospital,* **Maryna** *watches,
then walks away.*

A baby is crying somewhere. The rhythmic sound of a heart beat.

Colin *answers the door.*

Jasmine   I'm wet as fuck.

Colin   It's not a good time.

Jasmine   Can I come in or what?

Colin   What?

Jasmine   Funny.

She walks past him into the house.

Colin   She's not back till late.

Jasmine	Never is these days. She's got a reception till nine, then a late meeting, checked with her secretary, went over, had an argument today, so I know.
Colin	You went to her work?
Jasmine	I'm not interested in her anyway that's not why I'm here.

She looks at the house.

	I hated it when you moved. That was my house. I loved that place. But this is so ... House and Garden. Yeah ... none of my mates are around got exams or whatever so I thought you'll be on your own and you could probably do with a laugh so I brought a bottle of tequila. And a spliff or two, or three.
Colin	I don't really smoke illegal drugs, it's sort of frowned on for –
Jasmine	You should.
Colin	For husbands of government ministers.
Jasmine	You should, given everything that's happened to you.
Colin	A drug habit? Right.
Jasmine	You lost your job.
Colin	I'll find something else.
Jasmine	To take?
Colin	A job.
Jasmine	You probably wanted kids but she's past it now.
Colin	Not really.
Jasmine	No she is, well past it, trust me.

Colin   I mean we don't want kids.

Jasmine   The house must feel empty, with you here, on your own all day.

She lights a cigarette.

Colin   You can't smoke inside, you know that.

Jasmine   She isn't here.

                     So. Why can't you get a job? Too old is it?

Colin   In their terms, and I've never been one of the city boys really. Never done that stuff.

Jasmine   What stuff?

Colin   Cars, booze, coke.

Jasmine   Strippers.

Colin   Exactly. Strippers. God.

A moment.

                     And you're right, it's not been the easiest of months for her either, so she tends to take it out on ... well ...

Jasmine   You.

Colin   People.

Jasmine   You. It's all got a bit bleak recently, hasn't it?

Colin   Why are you here?

Jasmine   I'm your fairy godmother.

She offers him a cigarette.

Colin   I don't smoke.

Jasmine   If you're gonna have a mid life crisis, better have a fucking good one. It won't kill you.

He takes one. She lights it.

She pours two shots of tequila.

> Bad things are happening. Let's stick our heads in the sand.

They drink.

Sarah *is in a restaurant with* **Carter**.

Carter   For me, a restaurant is never about who will be here, but who certainly won't. And there are a lot of people who certainly won't be here. The wine's excellent, the meat isn't local which in London is a good thing, the service is eight out of ten. The cheese. Well, the cheese is something to write home about. Dear mother I have just tasted the most delightful cambozolla –

She gives him the sheets of paper.

> Oh.

> Straight to business. Thank you.

Sarah   Why don't you tell me what they are?

Carter   Well. They are ... results. Of some tests. Photocopies of the originals I think. It's a preliminary report by Robert Crannock ... your father yes?

Sarah   Why did you send them?

Carter   Me?

> No I didn't send them. I don't know anything about them.

The waiter comes over and pours some wine. **Sarah** *drinks straight away.*

Sarah   Alright well, why *might* someone ...

Carter   Why *might* someone have sent them?

Sarah   Exactly, yes, let's *imagine*.

Carter   Well these are signed by your father, the results of a project he did for the largest airline in the UK, oh hang on that's my company isn't it? Yes I remember this, a project over twenty years to investigate whether emissions from aircraft would have any lasting impact on the environment. Now this report seems to suggest that clearly, yes. Yes.

A huge impact.

These emissions would prove disastrous, for the world.

Sarah   Right. That's what he thinks.

Carter   But that wasn't his conclusion Sarah. Not at the time.

For twenty years, his public reports said the opposite. That burning fuel, and carbon emissions, would have little or *no effect*. It was one of the main factors in the expansion of the industry. So the question we ... sorry. Not me. The question you have to ask yourself is why would he do that? For twenty years.

When he knew the truth. Why would he lie?

Of course, everyone makes mistakes, we don't mind it took him twenty years to work it out, but if it were revealed that he knew *all the time* ... in green circles he's a god ... if this came out, his reputation would collapse.

And you're his daughter. Perhaps it would rub off on you.

I presume he was paid. I wonder how much?

Sarah *smiles.*

Sarah   Yes.

Carter   Yes?

Sarah   You're right. The public should know. I'll give the report to the press in the morning.

Carter   You will.

Sarah   Absolutely. And thank you, because this is a lovely restaurant, the wine is delicious, and especially for this, because I think my father deserves whatever he gets.

Carter   Really?

Sarah   You should've done your research. I hate him.
I'm more than happy to disown him publicly. Any excuse.

                   So sorry, John – no more runways.

She drinks from the wine.

Carter   I like the way you hold the glass. By the stem.
It's impressive. You're wasted.

Sarah   Not yet.

Carter   In politics, I meant.

Carter *takes the papers off her.*

                   You'll forgive the attempt? This sort of thing normally works on politicians. They get scared. Because most politicians are geeks, as you know Sarah. That's why they're so ugly.

The waiter arrives again.

                   But you.

You're not ugly at all. You're ... striking. Intelligent. So what are you doing?

What do you want?

Sarah   What do I want?

Carter   To eat.

Sarah   Oh.

Carter   I've done my best. It didn't work.

So, let's relax now, eat, drink.

Enjoy ourselves. Make a night of it.

Let's talk like men do.

The sound of a baby in the womb.

A young doctor, **Tim**, *is standing with* **Freya**.

Tim   We've run all the tests. I'm pleased to say, it's perfectly healthy.

Freya   I've been smoking. And drinking. I fell over in the bath.

Tim   She's fine.

Freya   Other mothers aren't like this.

Tim   Women often go through many feelings, but when you give birth –

Freya   You should get rid of it. The baby. Before it's too late. Ow!

Tim   It's not possible.

Freya   You do it all the time.

Tim   Not in these circumstances. She's too advanced.

Freya   If I was a cave woman, I could do it myself. Punch myself in the stomach.

	Or wait till it was born and hide it or bury it or something. Maybe I will. I thought this was civilised. I thought I had rights.
Tim	We are civilised. You do have rights. But at this stage, so does your daughter. Is someone picking you up?
Freya	I'm on my own. There isn't anyone. I'm staying here. I need to stay here.
Tim	We don't have room.
Freya	Sign a piece of paper and it's done – what?
Tim	What's really the matter?
Freya	I keep on telling you, there's something wrong.
Tim	Not with the baby?
Freya	I was out all day, I saw so many people and none of them cared. Are you a good doctor?
Tim	Are you a good patient?
Freya	Good patients would tell you their names.
Tim	I'm Tim.
Freya	Hello.
Tim	Hello Freya.
Freya	Oh, you know.
Tim	Found your wallet in your bag. Now all we need is an address.
Freya	Good hands.
Tim	Thanks.
Freya	I bet you keep your girlfriend happy.
Tim	Boyfriend actually.

Freya	Boyfriend right, I bet you wouldn't leave him by himself if he was having a baby.
Tim	Hard to say.
Freya	I'm not very happy at the moment. Brave face, but I'm struggling. You should let me stay.
Tim	Freya I can't unless you're in for a ... Do you want to see her?
Freya	Who?
Tim	Your daughter.
Freya	No.
Tim	If you see her, you can stay the night. That's the deal.

Tim *smiles*.

Freya	You're just like my husband.
Tim	In what way?
Freya	He's always smiling too, like nothing's wrong.

She winces with pain.

Steve *looks, very seriously, at* **Robert**.

Steve	It's a nice house.
Robert	Jealous.
Steve	Not really.
Robert	Small flat you've got. She finds it claustrophobic.
Steve	Is that what she said?
Robert	What do you think? Is she happy? With the house? Is she happy? With you?

	These are the questions. Point is, you don't know. What do you do Steve?
Steve	I'm sure she mentioned it.
Robert	Of course, but – I want you to be proud of it, Steve. I want you to declare it.
Steve	I'm a writer.
Robert	You're a writer. Good. Of?
Steve	Books. Sort of trivia books.
Robert	Sort of trivia books. That's right. What sort of trivia books?
Steve	For the Christmas market mainly, they're like stocking fillers.
Robert	And what do they like, fill the stocking with. What are they called?
Steve	The latest one was 'Fifty Shit Things About Britain'.
Robert	Fifty Shit Things About Britain. Wow. Steve. Wow. That's what you think? That Britain's shit.
Steve	Yeah, nothing to be proud of really.
Robert	Well I don't know, there's always your book.
Steve	We're working on a sequel actually, for this year.
Robert	Another Fifty Shit Things About Britain?
Steve	Fifty Shitter Things About Britain.
	They sell very well.
	The first bought the flat.
	This one's for Emily.

Robert   Emily?

Steve   . . .

Robert   Tell me some of your shit things.

Steve   Look, this isn't the point, I'm not here to chat –

Robert   Why not? Are you staying? Tonight?

Steve   You said a hotel.

Robert   There isn't one, and it's terrible anyway. Stay here.

Steve   No.

Robert   Why not? Scared?

Steve   It doesn't feel right.

Robert   What does that mean, 'doesn't feel right'?

Steve   To stay under your roof.

Robert   You don't know me.

Steve   I know what you did to them.

Robert   What I *did* to them. I didn't *do* anything. I said things. I told them the truth. *Did something,* sounds like you're implying I hit them.

Steve   No.

Robert   Or fucked them something like that. You're not implying something like that are you?

Steve   Of course not.

Robert   Then watch your fucking language.

Choose better words.

Stay. And we'll talk. We'll find the time. Later on. Yes?

Steve   Okay.

Robert   Good. Now, tell me why Britain's so shit.

Jasmine *and* **Colin** *have wine and are quite stoned.*

Jasmine   I feel so fucking aimless Colin, I want to go
                  where I want, do what I like, spend money,
                  I want to shout all the time. Cos it's bullshit,
                  just everyone, isn't it? Pushing emails
                  around, shall we meet? Shall we have a pre
                  meet? How about Thursday? I'm busy
                  Thursday, well how about we meet to work
                  out when's good, let's pencil that in, fucking
                  about on facebook, events, messages,
                  profiles, pretending to have friends, and I
                  don't mind but none of it's *achieving*
                  anything, it's one big 'general meeting', just
                  chatter, and when it all fucks up, which it
                  will, just statistically, historically, when it all
                  goes pear shaped, they'll be full of regrets. 'I
                  should've slept with him, I should've gone
                  there, done that while I had the chance'.
                  And I never want regrets Colin so while I still
                  can I'm gonna fuck some shit up.

Colin   I've never done that.

Jasmine   What?

Colin   Fucking ... shit ... or ...

Jasmine   Oh Colin.

Colin   I've found for the sake of dignity it's better to
                  stay away from the ... shit.

Jasmine   We have to sort you out.

Colin *lets out a long strange depressing sigh.*

Sarah *and* **Carter** *in a bar – more relaxed now.*

Cocktails and a night time view over London.

Sarah I have a fundamental belief in the role of government. I'm very clear about that.

Carter Sarah, it's wonderful your clarity.

Sarah And we're very different you and me.

Carter Different in many ways, I'm not denying that, I'm simply saying that with your skills, contacts, your background, you don't know how much you're worth.

Sarah I'm not interested in money.

Carter A thousand a day, possibly more.

Sarah It's not what motivates me.

Carter I know I know, okay, but the improved quality of life that's something else. I spend my evenings with my children. Do you spend your evenings with your children?

Sarah I don't have any children.

Carter You don't have any children alright, do you see much of your husband?

Sarah Enough.

Carter Enough?

He smiles – you see?

Sarah We're going through a … thing at the moment it's not … oh.

Carter This is what I mean.

Sarah Fuck. What am I doing? I'm telling you about my *marriage* why am I telling you about that? Jesus. Shut up Sarah.

Carter We're just talking.

Sarah *drinks her Mojito.*

But alright so quality of life, that's not a factor either, because there are important things you care about. I understand. Targets, limits, carbon trading, an international agreement. How's all that going by the way? Cos these days I don't hear so much about it.

Sarah   There's a lot of momentum to get something done.

Carter   Momentum.

Sarah   Yes. . . . I know I know alright.

Sarah *grabs a waiter.*

Can I get another Mojito?

He goes.

Carter   Come on Sarah, you like things to *happen*. You know really that the solution will lie in utilising the market. Technology and innovation.

Sarah   Carbon ingesting algae you mean?

Carter   Carbon –

Sarah   An orbiting umbrella.

Carter   Sarah, you're being / naughty.

Sarah   No no, my favourite – turning the moon into a huge solar panel.

Carter   That's kind of how innovation *works*. It's *new*? If people will pay, the world will change, fast. The internet existed for ten years, no one had it, but as soon as it could do adverts it went in every home.

Sarah   The environment is longer term, less quantifiable, without government incentivising industry there won't / be any commercial activity.

Carter	Sarah, *Sarah!* You could be doing so much more than incentivising. This is what I'm saying. There aren't many people around like you. If you were in business you could solve environmental issues right now, you could save lives and build economies and you could do it quickly. And then after work you'd go home to your big house, your happy husband, and do what you like. Concerts, painting, cooking.
Sarah	I used to like cooking.
Carter	What's your husband's name?
Sarah	Colin.
Carter	Colin? Right. Colin?

They both smile.

	Right.
Sarah	He's an amazing man.
Carter	I'm sure he is.
Sarah	But when I come in these days he just looks at me.
Carter	Because you're killing yourself with this half-arsed government when you're capable of so much more. He knows it. I know it.
Sarah	Well ...
	We'll have to wait and see.
Carter	Wait for what?
Sarah	The next election, see where we are.
Carter	That could be three years.
Sarah	Slowly slowly –
Carter	Why wait?

Sarah	You mean …
Carter	Come to us in the new year.
Sarah	I thought we were talking theoretically.
Carter	No.
Sarah	You want me to work for you.
Carter	Well actually Sarah, if you came across, I would be working for you.

She looks at him.

Proper salary, resources, investment, whatever you want. An expense account. Leading the field. Clean up the industry, from the inside. You tell us what to do.

Sarah	This is an offer?
Carter	A great big offer. You get what you want.
Sarah	Yes.
Carter	And so do we.

They look at each other.

Sarah   You're a clever boy.

She drinks. This is the deal.

Carter   The things you could do Sarah. So much bigger than planes and runways.

Robert, **Steve** *and* **Mrs Andrews** *are having dinner.*

Robert   Did you fly here Steve?

Steve   I didn't have much choice.

Robert *looks at him.*

Robert   You haven't read my books have you?

Steve   I had a look today, while I was waiting.

Robert   You had a *look?*

Steve   A skim, yes.

Robert   They aren't difficult, even Mrs Andrews managed them.

Steve   Your books aren't why I'm here.

Robert   Mrs Andrews, let me explain. Steve is worried about his wife. Now I haven't spoken to any of my daughters for twenty years. They don't like me, they're doing their own things – My eldest is the environment secretary. My youngest is at university. And Freya. What she does I don't know. She's pregnant, does that count?

Steve   She's a teaching assistant.

Robert   Yes, she helps deaf children or something, but quite strangely one evening, Steve got home and found his wife had gone. Where? Well he eventually discovered that she had got on a train and come up to Scotland, to talk to her dad. And yes. We spoke. You gave her fruit cake.

Mrs Andrews Aye.

Robert   Very appropriate in retrospect, because after she got home, she wouldn't tell her husband what we spoke about. He knew where she'd been, but Freya refused to talk. She wouldn't even say why she went in the first place. I presume she's become unhappy. Confused.

Steve   She hardly leaves the flat anymore, she cries at night.

Robert   Right, so then even more strangely, Steve decides to fake a business trip and come and talk to me himself. Not realising of course

	that if he needs to do that then there's much bigger issues at stake.
Steve	Like what?
Robert	Like not what I said to her.
Steve	Okay.
Robert	But why she won't talk to you. Why you're sneaking up here without telling her.
Steve	I need to know what's happening.
Robert	I'm in two minds as to what to say, Mrs Andrews. Steve's come all this way. But do I betray the trust of my daughter, and get involved or do I keep my mouth shut, for once?

They look at each other.

	The problem is Steve, that it is, in fact, all about my books. If you want an answer, you'll have to understand some science. You'll have to listen. And it won't be humorous. It's very interesting, but there aren't any *laughs*. Can you deal with that?
Steve	Go on.
Robert	Everything in the planet is co-dependent. It exists in ever changing, ever evolving balance much like a gigantic organism itself. Did you get that far with the books?
Steve	Yes / I did.
Robert	Species live and die and evolve and the planet evolves too through cycles of hot and cold and responding to the demands of life, and life responds to the demands of the planet. But the problem is /
Mrs Andrews	Global warming.

Robert	You see, there's a keen brain under all that – Global warming, yes. You know how that works. Of course you do. You've seen Blue Peter. And people draw their graphs, they show the rise in temperature, they show a small but steady rise, they say it can be limited, you know by how much?
Steve	A couple of degrees?
Robert	Two degrees yes, as long as we recycle, do you recycle Steve?
Steve	Yes.
Robert	And insulate our homes, I expect you've done that too.
Steve	Looked into it –
Robert	Of course you have I'm sure you've got a bag for life, and all that makes you feel better I know but it's a complete waste of time because the global climate has never been interested in two degree anything. If we look at geological records of historical climate change, the onset of the last ice age for instance, we see there is no steady climb, no year-by-year increase. There is in fact a relatively stable climate system, and then something happens, the system is stretched and in a moment, it collapses and changes, in hundreds not thousands of years. You understand?
Steve	…
Robert	Let's imagine this house is a planet. What regulates the climate?
Steve	The thermostat?
Robert	Mrs Andrews. When the house is too hot she opens windows, when it's too cold she

switches on the heating. She brings in new material to eat or drink, and she removes the waste when I'm done. She cleans the air and the ground and she regulates my life, don't you? We are symbiotic, she would not exist without me. I couldn't live without her.

Steve   Right.

Robert   But she's very unhappy at the moment Steve. Because when the population is doubled like this, her systems are stretched. The house gets hotter, quicker, food and drink are consumed at twice the rate, the floor is twice as dirty. She's under pressure, but is there a steady increase in her anger? Can you detect a slow rise in her temperament? No. She's stable, she's holding it together. But there will come a day, if you stay too long Steve, when the system's been stretched too far, and she'll snap. Suddenly she'll take away your sofa, she'll hide the food, leave the heating on, steal your phone and spit in your drink, she'll do everything in her power to remove the problem. To remove you. And she'll succeed Steve, you'll be gone, because she's stronger than any of us.

We were part of system, a relationship, and we abused it. The world will be fine in the end, and it knows what it wants. It wants to get rid of us.

Mrs Andrews   The end of humanity.

Steve *looks at them.*

Steve   Can we get back to Freya?

Robert   You don't believe me?

Steve   I don't see how it's relevant.

Robert   The end of humanity not relevant?

Steve   To what we're talking about, no.

Robert   Mrs Andrews. He doesn't believe me.

                      You think I'm a strange old man.

A pause.

Robert *stands up, goes to* **Steve**, *grabs him.*

Robert   Up.

Steve   What?

Robert   We're going.

Steve   Where?

Robert   The end of humanity. We're going to see it.

Jasmine *and* **Colin** *are smoking a spliff.*

Jasmine   I'm not wearing underwear.

                      I never do.

Colin   Uncomfortable.

Jasmine   It makes life that bit more exciting. You
                      should try it.

Colin   I don't think it's the same with men.

Colin *stares. Fixed. Empty.*

Nothing for a moment.

Jasmine *looks at him.*

He's blank.

Jasmine   Colin!

                      What's gonna change?

She pokes him.

                      Come on!!!

                      What's *happening!?*

She pokes him.

Pokes him again.

Keeps on poking him.

Poke poke.

He looks at her.

Then he stands up.

What?

What?

Have I pissed you off now?

Goes to the CD player. Picks a CD. Puts it on.

What are you doing?

The Arcade Fire – 'Rebellion (Lies)'. It plays.

What's this?

Colin   Arcade Fire.

Jasmine   Okay, yeah I remember them.

Colin *is standing moving a bit.*

Colin   Freya gave it to me one Christmas.

Used to play it in the car.

Colin *starts to dance to it, very awkwardly. He knows the words, but is not used to moving his body.*

Jasmine   Oh.

My.

God.

Colin   You like it?

Jasmine   Er ... I ...

Jasmine *is amazed.*

Colin *dances.*

       Yeah.

Colin *sings along, loudly now.*

> *'Sleeping is giving in,*
> *no matter what the time is.*
> *Sleeping is giving in,*
> *so lift those heavy eyelids.*
>
> *People say that you'll die*
> *faster than without water.*
> *But we know it's just a lie,*
> *scare your son, scare your daughter.'*

As he goes he grows in confidence, he starts to let go. There is a kind of beauty to it.

Jasmine *is laughing and smoking.*

Carter *pays for the drinks at the bar.*

Carter   You look different Sarah.

Sarah   What?

Carter   You look younger.

Sarah *smiles.*

Colin *dances with things in the room. Bashes around. Starts to go crazy. No ironic moves. He means it.*

He pulls **Jasmine** *up. Dances with her, sings to her. She can't believe it.*

> *'People say that your dreams*
> *are the only things that save ya.*
> *Come on baby in our dreams,*
> *we can live on misbehaviour.*
>
> *Every time you close your eyes*
> *Lies, lies!*
> *Every time you close your eyes*
> *Lies, lies!*

> *Every time you close your eyes*
> *Lies, lies!*
> *Every time you close your eyes*
> *Lies, lies!*
>
> *Every time you close your eyes.*

Jasmine   You're mental!

Colin   *Every time you close your eyes.*
Every time you close your eyes.
Every time you close your eyes.'

He lets himself go completely.

Freya *and* **Tim**. *The music playing underneath.*

Freya   She's not kicking anymore.
She seems happy. I think she likes you.

She smiles.

Maybe she could be a doctor, do something good.

He smiles.

Tim   Back in a minute.

He goes out.

Carter *and* **Sarah** *are outside in the rain under an umbrella.*

Colin   *People try and hide the night.*
Underneath the covers.
People try and hide the lie.
Underneath the covers.

Come and hug your lovers
Underneath the covers.
Come and hug your lovers

Underneath the covers.

Hide it from your brothers.
Underneath the covers.
Come and hug your lovers
Underneath the covers.

Carter   There's a fifty. For the cab.

Sarah   It won't be that much.

Carter   Buy something for your husband.

Sarah *smiles, gets in a cab and drives off through the city.*

Colin *continues to dance and mime along with the words.*

Colin   *'People say that you'll die*
                    faster than without water,
                    but we know it's just a lie,
                    scare your son, scare your daughter,

Jasmine *is going as mad as he is. They dance close*

                    Scare your son, scare your daughter.
                    Scare your son, scare your daughter.'

She kisses him suddenly.

He stops her. Stands back.

They look at each other as the music continues to play.

Jasmine *sits. Relights the spliff.*

Colin *listens to the music a bit, then fades it down and switches it off.*

We hear the sound of the storm outside.

Robert *is walking with* **Steve** *up to a tree.*

Robert   There's a nest in this tree. Redwings,
                    beautiful patterning. They were the reason
                    I moved here. I found the birds, bought the
                    house nearby.

Steve   I'm asking about / Freya.

Robert   The birds were endangered and climate
                    change was the cause apparently. So I
                    thought, they will be my barometer. Like the
                    ravens in the tower, when they leave, it's
                    over. They said rising temperatures were
                    driving them elsewhere. What do you think?

Steve   Doesn't feel warm right now.

Robert   Well exactly, how could you know it was the air temperature? If you want to understand these things, you have to look at the entire system, the mountains, the animals, the air, the sea, it's infinitely complicated Steve, but that's what I do, I sit in that shed and I try to see the future.

Steve   Just you and your shed.

Robert   Every model suggests things are going to be worse than anyone imagines. I've seen something terrible,

Steve   You're the only one who's noticed.

Robert   People say they want the truth – facts, and figures, but actually they want to be told it can be avoided, with minimum effort. When Neville Chamberlain came back from Hitler. He said he had a peace treaty, said he could *trust* this obviously evil man. Why did he believe it? Why did *we* believe it? Because we had to, or we'd be facing untold horrors. Always Steve, faith will come before truth. That's who we are.

Steve   Freya's read your books, she knows what you think, so why did she come all the way up here?

Robert   They all know what I think. Best way to reduce the carbon footprint?

Steve   What?

Robert   No foot. You want to be green?

Steve   Okay –

Robert   Hold your breath. The planet can sustain
                    about one billion people. We currently have
                    six billion. So in the next hundred years it
                    will balance the books. You understand?

Steve   I don't –

Robert   Five billion people wiped from the face of
                    the earth in a single lifetime. Mass migration
                    away from the equator, world wars,
                    starvation . . .

Steve   And Freya –

Robert   Freya came to ask my advice about children.

Steve   And what did you say?

Robert   You have to understand –

Steve   What did you *say?*

Robert   I told her that her child will regret she was
                    ever born. Hate her mother for forcing her
                    into a terrible world.

                    I told her to do whatever it takes.

                    I told her to kill it.

Steve *looks at him. Horrified.*

Tim *is operating the ultrasound on* **Freya**.

We see a very blurred image. Of something. Faint sound of the womb.

Tim   There. Can you see?

Freya   No.

Tim   Look.

Freya   I can't see anything.

Steve *and* **Robert**.

Steve   You told her to kill it.

Robert   Yes.

Steve   Emily.

Robert	It's a / foetus.
Steve	We're calling her Emily and I've no idea what's going to happen, but she's there, and growing, and she's my child too, not just Freya's, she's much more important than your theories ... your fucking *birds*.
Robert	It's not just theory / it's
Steve	You had no right. No right to say that to her.
Robert	It's the truth.
Steve	You listen! To me.
Robert	The birds? You want to know about / the birds?
Steve	For once, you listen. You had no right to say that to her. Do you understand?
Robert	Steve!
Steve	No –
Robert	The birds had gone before I even moved in.

Steve *moves away, to avoid hitting him.*

Robert	It's Weimar time, it's Cabaret, across the world. You feel it, we all do. We know there's nothing to be done, so we're dancing and drinking as fast as we can. The enemy is on its way, but it doesn't have guns and gas this time, it has wind and rain, storms and earthquakes.
Steve	Just shut up. / Shut up.
Robert	This isn't theory. This is *death*, this is *loss* and *pain*. Freya's not the first to suffer, and she won't be the last.
Steve	She's beautiful and clever, but she's not strong, she came up here for help. She wanted her dad to make her feel better.

Robert   Then she came to the wrong person.

Steve   What did she do?
                      What did she do when you told her?

Robert   The world as it is, a disgrace.
                      The world as it will be, unbearable.

Steve   I have to get back. I couldn't get through to
                      her at home. She's gone somewhere.

Robert   You can't get back now.

Steve   She might be killing my baby, so –

Steve *leaves.*

Robert   She had to know the truth.
                      It's better it never lived.

Tim *is still trying with the ultrasound.*

Freya   You aren't what you seem.

Tim   I'm sorry?

Freya   I saw you. Through the glass. Talking to the
                      nurse. Ow! It's started again.

Tim   I just need to find the . . .

Freya   I teach deaf children at school. Part of my
                      job.

Tim   Really?

Freya   Means I lip read.

Tim   Oh.

Freya   Mad bitch.
                      Waste of time.
                      Then you both laughed.

Tim   It was a joke.

Freya   No. It's what you think. And it doesn't
                      matter except I thought you were the good
                      thing, you were the last glimmer.

And then you went out.

Aghh!

She hates you now.

On the screen is a very clear image of a foetus.

Tim   I've had a long day. I'm sorry.
             But look.
             There she is.

             Things'll seem better.
             She'll make a difference, won't she?
             When she's here.

Freya   Yes.

             She will.

             She will make a difference.

The foetus is on the screen. Kicking.

Its mouth moves and we hear a small voice.

Foetus   Mummy?

Freya   It spoke.

Tim   What?

Freya   It moved its mouth.

Tim   It's just –

Freya   No. I lip read. It's speaking.

Foetus   Mummy?

             Mummy?

             Help.

             Help me.

Sound of the womb getting louder and louder.

Sounds like an earthquake.

Mummy?

Shaking.

The foetus turns its head to face us and screams.

Blackout.

End of Act Three.

Interval.

Act Four

Prologue

1991

Robert *is watching television in the dark, drunk.*

A door opens onto a hall where bags are packed.

Sarah *comes in.*

Sarah   I've packed enough for a week, for all of us, but we'll have to come back for the rest at some point, if you're serious about all this. There's too much, there's all the baby things, the nappies, the sheets, the toys, the bottle, I mean I can't fit the cot in my car, we'll have to get a van or something, I don't know, if you're serious.

        I don't know if you are serious but if you mean what you said, I'm going right now.

Robert   With you I tried.

Sarah   What?

Robert   Everyone had said if you have a child you'll change, you'll know what to do, everything will fall into place, and so I went into the hospital on the day you were born and there was your mum sat in the bed, and she gave you to me, to hold, and I looked at you, and I waited.

        For that moment when I would feel like a father.

        The moment everyone spoke about, when I would love you, completely, above anything else. But it wasn't happening.

        I looked over at your mum and she smiled. It had happened for her.

I looked down at you.

Still nothing.

So I looked up at your mum and smiled back, and right then, I started pretending. A few years later we had Freya, and Jasmine, and every moment, all the time, I wasn't a father. I never felt it.

But now she's gone, now your mother's dead, there's no reason to pretend. She was the one I loved. Just her. Yes. I'm serious.

Sarah   What work?

Robert   What?

Sarah   You said you had work to do, that you needed to focus.

Robert   I've got to *stop pretending*.

Sarah *looks at him. Very upset. Holding it in.*

Sarah   So every time you've hugged me and talked to me at bedtime, and drove me to university –

Robert   Yes.

Sarah   All the hours we talked, all that was –

Robert   You believed it at the time.
That's what mattered.

A baby is crying.

Sarah   I left Jasmine with Freya.

Coldly, **Sarah** *goes over and kisses* **Robert**.

Robert   You look like your mother. That's what I can't deal with. You all look just like her.

Sarah *exits, leaving the door open.*

The baby cries.

Robert   Don't have children.
                      Don't ever bring me grandchildren.

He turns back into the room, facing away from the door.

We hear the ten-year-old **Freya**'s *voice.*

Freya   Daddy?

Robert   Go away.

Freya   I found this dress. I think it was Mum's. Can
                      I have it? I like the flowers.

Robert   Don't touch a thing.

Freya   Daddy?

Robert   Leave me alone.

Freya   Daddy?

Robert   No!

Freya   I'm pregnant.

Robert *turns. Facing him is thirty-year-old* **Freya**, *pregnant, holding the dress.*

                      What do I do?

Growing sound of white noise again, like a rumble, maybe like water, building up into . . .

Thomas Hood

Early in the morning.

Light just on **Freya** *in her hospital bed. She gets out of bed fully dressed, and puts her bag on.*

She puts her headphones in and presses play, and sets out.

Maryna, *the Polish cleaner from before, sees* **Freya** *and starts singing 'I Am Not a Robot' by Marina and the Diamonds.*

Freya *leaves the hospital with* **Maryna,** *and passes a group of men smoking outside,* **Freya** *steals one.*

The man steals his cigarette back.

Freya   Oh.

Freya *walks down the road into the city, with* **Maryna,** *and picking up some other commuters behind her. They walk with her, singing.*

As **Freya** *starts to become happier, the commuters stop and lift her up and around, as she sings.*

They put her down and they run – into Covent Garden! Various street performers appear, including a robot performer, a juggler, a few tourists, and some kids. **Freya** *plays with them all, hopscotch, eating fruit from a stall, dancing with a waiter.*

Everyone dances. A marching band appears, some people dressed as animals. People on TV in shop windows joining in. Everything moving. Signs, shops, the sun!

Huge lights, glitter from the ceiling, or a newspaper seller throws her free papers in the air. Ushers dancing and singing in the audience.

Peter *appears, looking for* **Freya.** *Everyone starts moving off, going about their normal boring business.* **Maryna** *goes home.*

The newspaper seller clears up her papers, slightly confused and leaves.

Freya *starts to text on her phone.*

Freya *is crying, and texting, she leans against a wall and sinks down to her knees.* **Peter** *taps her on the shoulder.*

Peter	Hello miss.
Freya	Oh / no.
Peter	Was that you singing?
Freya	You're supposed to be at home.
Peter	I know but I got bored it's all box sets and nothing in your flat, led me to a complete feeling of apathy sat around like that, I see what you meant now, so I thought I'd come and find you, you don't mind do you? You look terrible. Not being rude but you look completely white. Like someone addicted to heroin. Or someone that's dead. What are you doing?

Dark clouds appear. White noise.

Freya	Nothing. Leave me alone.

She gets up and walks off, still texting.

He waits for a moment, then follows her.

The white noise turns into radio in a cab office. **Steve** *is arguing with* **Mrs Andrews**.

Mrs Andrews	Forty minutes
Steve	No, I've been here all night, I'm not waiting any longer.
Mrs Andrews	Well I'm sorry but they said the driver's on his way and a Ford Focus only goes so fast in this weather.
Steve	Ford Focus? Jesus.
Mrs Andrews	It's no bad thing you learn a lesson. You may be worried, you may want to get home but you can't beat nature. You can't hold back the tide.

Steve   Well we can.

Mrs Andrews   What?

Steve   That's exactly what the Thames Barrier does. Stops the tide coming in. We build tunnels, we fly, we go to the moon, of course you can beat nature –

Steve *receives a text message. He reads it.*

                   We can do what we want, and right now I want my fucking taxi. So.

He looks up.

                   Forty minutes, you're sure?

White noise.

Sarah *has made breakfast in the kitchen.*

Colin *comes in.*

Sarah   Late night?

Colin   Can you not?

Sarah   I made some tea.

She puts it on the side.

Colin   Shouldn't you have gone by now?

Sarah   I want to talk.

Colin   I know I know, we made a mess, we'll tidy up. Don't worry, go.

Sarah   I've made a decision.

Colin   A decision?

Sarah   I've had an offer.

Colin   Right ... you're ...

Sarah   I'm going to resign. Take a new job.

Colin   Look, I've got a headache.

Sarah   In the commercial sector. I'll start in the
new year.
I was. Wrong. Colin.
I'm sorry.
You come first.

Colin *smiles*.

What? That's funny?

Colin   You're going to work for a company?

Sarah   A multinational company, position on the
board maybe. It pays well, the hours are
better.

Colin   You used to throw things.

Sarah   I ... what?

Colin   You used to throw things through windows.

Sarah   I'm sorry Colin you're not making sense.

Colin   You'd bunk off work, go into town and shout
your lungs out. Protesting against whatever
it was, I'd come and pick you up round the
corner.

Sarah   Well thankfully I've grown up so –

Colin   Wearing those dresses, you used to get in the
car, your face would be red with shouting,
and your hair down, you'd have thrown
something at some bank, or the police and
you'd jump in the car and say drive – just
drive, and we'd speed off, like a film, in my
Volvo.

Sarah   You hated all that.

Colin   At least we argued about things that
mattered.

Now you want to be on the board.

Sarah	I thought you'd be pleased. I thought you'd at least talk to me about it.
Colin	Look.
Sarah	What?
Colin	We hate each other.
Sarah	I don't hate you.

They look at each other.

It's Jasmine.

Colin	No.
Sarah	She's been talking, making you like this, while I'm the one mopping up, dealing with her fucking ...
Colin	Just fun.
Sarah	Her *vomit,* I take her to the doctor, pay her rent, credit cards and –
Colin	It's not Jasmine.

A moment. **Sarah** *picks up the tea, offers it.*

Sarah	Are you going to drink your tea?
Colin	You should go. You'll be late.

Jasmine *comes down, in her nightdress, smoking a cigarette.*

Jasmine	Tea! Great.

She takes it off **Sarah** *and drinks.*

Sarah	You can put that out Jasmine. You know not to smoke inside.
Jasmine	I'm not smoking.
Sarah	This is my house.
Jasmine	Yeah, it looks like you.
Sarah	What?

Jasmine	Dated. Subsidence, dry rot. Cracks beginning to show. In desperate need of redecoration.
Sarah	I've done everything for you and you're ...
Jasmine	Do you know what comes before part B?
Sarah	What?
Jasmine	Part A!
Sarah	For Christ's –
Jasmine	Come on that was funny.
Sarah	You're like Dad. Just like him.
Jasmine	Wouldn't know would I?
Sarah	Colin can we have a conversation ...
Jasmine	We should take you shopping today Colin, find you some new clothes, sort you out, what do you think?

Sarah's *phone gets a text message. She picks up the phone, looks at it, puts it in her pocket – looks at* **Colin**.

Colin	Good luck with your job.

Sarah *goes, upset.*

Jasmine	We so got it on last night – alright, we didn't exactly get it on but you were a bit frisky for a minute or two – alright maybe you weren't a bit *frisky*, but your heart was going like bang bang bang, bang bang – alright maybe not bang bang bang but –
Colin	I nearly told her I wanted a divorce.
Jasmine	Oh.
Colin	Just now.
Jasmine	Because of us? Cos you're great Colin but I don't know if I want a proper relationship.

Colin   Don't be stupid Jasmine.
                   I'm serious.

Jasmine   . . .

Colin   So what do you think?

Jasmine   A divorce? Don't know.

Jasmine's *phone gets a text. She picks it up. Shrugs.*

                   Things change.

A hint of white noise. **Jasmine** *reads her text.*

Steve, *tired and unshaven, comes into the living room and picks up his bag.* **Robert** *is there.*

Robert   Did you call her?

Steve   She's texted. She wants to meet.

Robert   Good, she wants to meet. Good.

Steve   You're right she'll have a difficult life.

Robert   Freya?

Steve   Emily. She'll not have the things we had,
                   maybe.

Robert   That's right.

Steve   The world could be terrible. It could be.

Robert   Yes.

Steve   But she'll be clever, like her mum, so that's
                   good, and she'll have a practical attitude
                   which comes from me. An intuition.

Robert   This isn't the point Steve.

Steve   I think it is. The point. I really think it is.
                   Even if things do get difficult, really tough,
                   like you said, the world'll be better with her
                   in it. She'll add something special.

Robert	Don't you think all fathers think this?
Steve	No, not all fathers. No.
Robert	. . .
Steve	And anyway this isn't the future, she's already there, thinking, learning. Sucking her thumb, listening.
Robert	You like things simple. I understand. Fair enough. You don't want to think about it.

Robert *laughs, sits down. The taxi beeps.*

Do what you want. Not my problem anymore.

Steve *picks up his bag, takes out a book and gives it to* **Robert**.

Steve	My book.
Robert	Your book.
Steve	There's something on page thirty-seven you'd recognise. It's about angry old men who think they're prophets and stand on street corners with signs, shouting at anyone who walks past.
Robert	Fascinating.
Steve	They want the world to end when they do.
Robert	Really?
Steve	And they smell.
Robert	What?
Steve	Because they're on their own, they smell, a bit, of piss.

Don't get up.

He leaves. **Robert** *sits in the chair. White noise grows.*

Tom's *phone rings. He's in his underwear, just woken up.*

Sarah *has arrived at work, and is trying to get through.*

Simon	The PM says half an hour this morning but only if it's important.
Sarah	Say it's vital.
Simon	Are you sure?
Sarah	Use that word when you tell him.
Simon	/ 'Vital'.
Tom	Hello?
Sarah	Tom. This is the secretary of state for energy and climate change we spoke yesterday, you came to visit.
Tom	How did you get my number?
Sarah	I've been thinking about what you said and I wondered if you'd be around for lunch.
Tom	Lunch?
Sarah	Yes. Today. Somewhere nice.
Tom	I've only just got up.
Sarah	That's fine. Get dressed. You've got a tie?
Tom	I'm a student.
Sarah	I'll send a car. He'll bring a tie. Half twelve?
Tom	How do you know where I live?
Sarah	44 Lonsdale Road.
Tom	Yeah but –
Sarah	Perfect. Half twelve. See you then.

She hangs up.

Simon	Minister, what are you doing?
Sarah	I'm cooking.

Freya *is walking down the street followed by* **Peter**, *walking behind her.*

Peter	Did you walk all the way here?
Freya	Yes.
Peter	Like Dick Whittington?
Freya	What?
Peter	It's a pantomime.
Freya	I know what it is. / Jesus.
Peter	I saw Dick Whittington at the Hexagon in Reading.
Freya	Peter –
Peter	It had Les Dennis in it. It was a bit embarrassing all round I thought. But anyway in that he walks to London and becomes Mayor. Maybe you'll become Mayor.
Freya	I've had enough. I want to stop.
Peter	Or perhaps you're here because of the earthquake.

She stops.

It's supposed to happen today.

Freya	I know, I know it's *supposed* to but –
Peter	Right so when it does you'll need a sidekick. Dick Whittington had a cat, I can be the cat?

She turns away from him.

Freya	I'm imagining you. The drink or the pills in hospital or some kind of paranoia, schizophrenia something like that, the blood rushing to my head.
Peter	There's a long history of earthquakes in the capital. One in 1580 killed two people and

made everyone think that it was Judgment Day.

Freya   Peter . . . / shut up.

Peter   Another one in 1931 originated in Yorkshire but made chimneys fall down in Clapham. The most recent was in 2008. They happen quite a lot.

Freya   You should be interested in girls or something.

Peter   I am.

Freya   I'm tired.

Peter   I am interested in girls or / something.

Freya   Why isn't there ever anywhere to sit down!?

She sits down on the ground.

They say when you give birth, the pain is unbearable. That's why women forget. Your skin tears, there's blood and there's shit and you scream and it feels like you're going to die.

She scratches at her stomach a bit.

Peter   You still got my flower?

She has the flower stuck in her bag.

Freya   I like it.

Peter   You should keep going miss.

Freya   Why?

Peter   I think you're nearly there.

That way.

Freya *stands and carries on.* **Peter** *smiles and follows.*

Liberty, on Carnaby Street.

Jasmine *sits with a Liberty Girl, waiting for* **Colin***.*

Jasmine	I'm not going to steal anything.
Liberty	
Jasmine	Do you have to wear all that make-up?
	You must be depressed working in a shop like this, standing here all the time, you look really depressed.
Liberty	This isn't just a shop.
Jasmine	What?
Liberty	This is Liberty.
Jasmine	But how much do you get paid?
Liberty	I'm sorry?
Jasmine	It's probably not much is it?
Liberty	What do you do?

Jasmine *shouts through the changing room.*

Jasmine	Colin! You know how to get dressed right?

No reply.

	You should break out, come with us, what's your name?
Liberty	Liberty.
Jasmine	That's the name of the shop I meant what's *your* name?
Liberty	It's my name as well.
Jasmine	Coincidence.
Liberty	Not really. I wanted to work here from when I was fourteen. I love this place, the people, the lighting. Most items cost well over two hundred pounds. I used to come here for

hours and walk around and touch things. Then when I was eighteen I applied for the job. I put Liberty on the form, as my name. I thought it would get their attention. I was right. When I got the job, I applied to deed poll, so my bank details would match. I wear this amount of make up so my skin tone goes exactly with the colour of the walls? And you'll notice my clothes co-ordinate with the posters, and the sign outside.

Jasmine   Well, *Liberty*, that's brilliant but we're drinking Ouzo and you should blow this off, come and have a laugh with us.

Liberty   You and your dad?

Jasmine   He's not my dad. We're together, out on the town, we're going to have it, what do you think?

She looks at **Liberty** *and smiles.*

Liberty   No thanks.

Jasmine   Can't believe you're called Liberty. What was your old name?

Liberty   Nicola.

Jasmine   I like Nicola.

Liberty   Nicola's shit. Liberty's better. What's your name?

Jasmine   Jasmine.

Liberty   Who called you that? Your mum or something?

Jasmine   . . .

Liberty   Jasmine doesn't mean anything. Liberty's better.

It means freedom.

Sarah, **Tom** *and* **Carter** *in a restaurant.*

Carter	How are you feeling today?
Sarah	I'm feeling really good, thank you.
Carter	Stronger constitution than the country you're running. Not many people can say that. Who's this?
Sarah	This is Tom.
Tom	Hi.
Carter	Work experience?
Sarah	Tom's a friend.
Carter	Hi Tom. Nice tie.
Tom	She said we were going somewhere posh.
Carter	Posh? Here? No. This isn't posh.
Sarah	I met Tom yesterday. He has family in Eritrea. Do you know where that is?
Carter	There are so many countries aren't there? Africa or something probably? We don't fly there, I know that.
Tom	The crops don't grow anymore. The temperature is rising year on year. The people, my family, they're getting to the point where either they move or they die.
Sarah	Tom doesn't really approve of your plans.
Carter	What are you doing Sarah?
Tom	You think your suit looks really good don't you?
Carter	It's not about what I think, actually, Tom, it's a fact. This suit is really impressive.

Sarah   Tom tried to blackmail me. He thought at the time Heathrow wasn't enough he heard I was due to make an announcement and he demanded a complete halt to air travel expansion. Now, I gave him hell because I don't like to be blackmailed. As you know. I told him I hadn't made up my mind.

Carter   Which turned out to be true.

Sarah   But speaking to my husband this morning, he mentioned how I used to throw things at the windows of large corporations like yours. As you know we're going through a difficult time at the moment but he seemed to think I was more attractive back then, and I could see what he meant.

Carter   Oh I get it, you're making a *point*, she's *using* you Tom. Well look, Africa's a pretty shit place to grow vegetables global warming or not, what with the sun and the desert and the *civil war*. Maybe your family should move, get away from it all on one of our nice big planes, or is that not the point you're making?

Sarah   I was reminded why I went into politics, Tom and I / aren't so different.

Carter   I know a fantastic therapist, Sarah, if that's what this is really / about.

Sarah   So I gave Tom a call, asked him to join us.

Carter   This thing with *teenagers* / it's *strange*

Sarah   Then I called the Prime Minister's office to bring forward the meeting.

Carter   The Prime Minister?

Sarah   I sat down with him and put forward my case.

Carter   You did.

Sarah   A total halt to expansion, guaranteed. No more runways, control, terminals, nothing, right across the country. I said he had to be firm, make a lasting decision. I told him a strong message on this would unite the government, and be popular with the country.

Carter   And what did he say?

Sarah   He's very green. He's got a wind turbine on his roof. Next week, we announce. It's over.

Carter *smiles at them.*

In Liberty

Colin *comes out from the dressing room. He's wearing a very expensive suit, shirt and tie, with new shoes. He's had a hair cut as well. He looks fantastic.*

Jasmine   Wow.

Colin   Is it alright?

Liberty   How does it feel?

Colin   Not sure. How much is it?

Liberty *gets out a calculator.*

Liberty   Well, with the suit, the shoes, the tie, the shirt. The cufflinks, the vest, the care cover, you'll want that, the socks, the laces …

                    Five thousand pounds and forty-four pence.

Colin   Oh my god.

Liberty   Perhaps your girlfriend would like something of her own?

Colin   She's not my girlfriend.

Liberty   She said she / was –

Colin	Is that what you told her?
Jasmine	No.
Colin	Jasmine!
Jasmine	Colin!
Colin	She's my wife's sister.
Liberty	Oh just your ... well ... that explains it then.
Jasmine	What?
Liberty	Why she's trying so hard.

A moment.

Anyway what do you think?

Shall we put it through?

Is it something you think you could own?

Sarah, **Tom** *and* **Carter**.

Carter	Tom, do you have a computer?
Tom	Yeah.
Carter	Phone?
Tom	Of course.
Carter	You drive a car?
Tom	And get to the point?
Carter	All of them developed for profit. It's how we progress. But Sarah thinks we've reached the first moment in human existence where we have to stop, and go backwards. She thinks this moment is entirely different to anything that's ever happened.
Tom	But the world *is* / different. It has limits.
Carter	There will be more air travel Tom. Because people want it. People have the right. To be free, to make their own choices.

Tom	What's more important, a stag weekend in Amsterdam or the entire nation of Tuvalu sinking underwater? Six flights a year to a second home, or starving families in Eritrea?
Carter	I admire the passion Tom, and clearly you're a bright boy with huge potential but is this really what you want to do? You could come with me in a minute, I'll show you round the office, I'll pay your university fees, and before long you'll be eating in restaurants like this, with beautiful people and respect and all the resources you need to protect the people you love. Or, you could end up serving in restaurants like this, on the edge, struggling financially, a slow crawl to last place. Sarah's just made the wrong decision, there are so many women like her, lonely, past it, no children but she needs a project, so now we're all her fucking children, stupid and careless and in need of protection, and that's fine, she's nothing, she'll be forgotten, but it's not too late for you Tom, what do you think?
Sarah	Tom's got what he wanted.
Tom	What?
Sarah	This is a good day for him.
Tom	This isn't / what I wanted.
Sarah	Like me, he just wants things to be fair.
Carter	So you're not enjoying the restaurant Sarah? Or the bar last night? Your big house? / Nice holidays?
Sarah	I'm not denying people their lifestyle but –
Tom	Why / not?

Sarah   There has to be a balance between –

Carter   You should've seen the salary we offered her. And we never ask twice so –

Sarah   I'd rather eat my own shit than work for you.

Carter   Sort of thing you'd actually do. And anyway –

A bit of bread hits **Carter**.

                   What.

Tom   Shut the fuck up.

Thrown by **Tom**, *who's standing up.* **Sarah** *smiles.*

Sarah   Good shot.

He throws another bit at **Sarah**.

Sarah   Hey.

Tom   No.

                   We shouldn't be flying at all.

Carter   Ah, now, you see?

Sarah   Tom.

Tom   No *expansion* still means thousands of flights every single day. You've all had your whole lives to sort out the planet, and you've done precisely nothing. Now, according to the best scientists, we've got about five years left before it's too late, so you'll forgive me if I don't wait for the next *election*, you'll understand if I'm *impatient*. Because while you continue to have conversations like this, in London restaurants, in government lobbies and Notting Hill gardens, while you show off your little wind turbines, and while you're talking and talking, you're still doing absolutely fuck all. And meanwhile, the clock is ticking, the ice caps are melting, people are dying and it's my generation who'll pay the price, long after you're both dead, so I think this is the turning point. Right now. I'm going to sleep with more sisters of elected politicians, I'm going to handcuff myself to railings, I'm going to attack police, issue bomb threats. Until something is done, something *real*, I'm going to add to the long and noble tradition of direct action.

He takes a plate and smashes it onto the floor.

There are children dying that shouldn't be dying. *Lifestyle?* Fuck your *lifestyle*.

He kicks over a chair.

Cunts. All of you. Are you embarrassed?

You should be.

Tom *leaves*. **Carter** *smiles*. **Sarah** *drinks her wine*.

A busker appears and starts playing.

Freya *is now walking with* **Peter** *by the Houses of Parliament.*

Freya   My dad says, in a few years, they'll look back, on the ruins of London, when the city's underwater, and the old people will say, do you remember walking down Oxford Street? The view from St Pauls? By that time there'll be heat waves, storms, even this earthquake might be caused by us they think. Something to do with ice sheets crashing into the sea. Decreasing amounts of sediment between the tectonic plates.

Peter   I think it's God.

Freya   What?

Peter   Don't you think if there is a God, he's pissed off? Like when you leave a mug in your room too long and it grows into this rank horrible green pus. You throw it away when that happens don't you? You get a new one. Start again.

Steve *is in Victoria station, a man in a polar bear costume approaches him. He is holding a bucket of money.*

Steve   I'm in a hurry.

Polar Bear   I'm dying.

Steve   Do you know where the tube is?

Polar Bear   I know my whole habitat is disappearing down the tube, I know that.

Steve   Right, excuse me.

Polar Bear   Melting icebergs, whole eco-systems eradicated, maybe you could spare a few pounds?

Steve   I don't have any change.

Polar Bear   I'll do a dance.

Steve   Can you get out of my way?

Polar Bear   It's a good dance.

Steve   Who are you?

The **Polar Bear** *reveals his face.*

Polar Bear   It's Rag week. Greenpeace.

Steve   Can you just / get out of the –

Polar Bear   Cheer up, might never happen.

Steve *struggles with the bear, pushes past and off.*

A **Young Man**, *dirty and sweaty runs up to* **Freya** *grabs her arm.*

Young Man   Please! Please.

Freya   Oh. You ... How was –

Young Man   I'm sorry but my kid! My kid's in hospital, I've just found out, I need the bus fare to get down the road, I don't have any ... change ... I'm sorry, I'm really in a hurry, I'm really sorry. Shit. Shit.

Freya   You asked me this yesterday.

Young Man   What?

Freya   About your kid. I gave you five pounds. You said exactly the same thing then.

Young Man   Oh. Right, yeah yeah.

Freya   You don't ... have a kid, do you?

The **Young Man** *looks at her – of course he doesn't. He runs off – the* **Polar Bear** *leaves as well. A rumble.*

Peter   Depressing, isn't it?

Come on.

Freya *looks at* **Peter**.

Freya   Peter. What's going on?

Peter   What?

Freya   You don't make sense, following me.

Peter   I register very high on the autism spectrum. It's the sort of thing I'd do.

Freya   You're not even that convincing. Shouldn't your voice have broken by now?

Peter   Yes, that's true, it should've broken by now.

Freya   Right. So. Peter. What's going on?

Peter   I think I have some kind of purpose. Maybe it's to do with the earthquake. Sometimes people imagine a figure who represents death, the bringer of bad news, a man who will guide them from this life into the next. I could be Peter, at the gates of heaven.

Freya   My version of death is a sullen fourteen-year-old boy with behavioural difficulties?

Peter   He takes many forms.

Freya *walks away, upset.*

Peter   Or I maybe I'm a herald.

Freya   What am I supposed to do?

Peter   Peter Rabbit. At the rabbit hole.

Freya   I don't know why I'm here, or where I am, I don't want the baby –

Peter   Miss –

Freya   – but I can't get rid of it, my family hate me, not a single friend has called me all week.

Peter   Miss –

Freya   I'm a fuck up, a fuck up, on my own. A complete fucking MESS.

She looks at her belly.

I don't want you! Little fucking . . .

She punches it.

Peter   Miss! I can feel it.

Freya   What?

Peter   It's time.

Freya   Peter, I've had enough!

Peter   I'm a carrier signal.

Freya   A what?

Peter   Someone wants to talk to you and they're using me to get through.

                    This is the moment when ... The time has
                    come. This is the moment.

Freya   The moment?

Peter *starts to remove his hoodie and his glasses.*

Peter   This is the moment when I ...

                    Who are you thinking of most?

                    The moment when I ...

                    Who do you think of all the time?

Freya   I don't –

Peter   Who are you thinking of right now?

Freya   Emily.

Peter   Emily, yes.

Peter *lets his hair down.*

Now revealed is a sixteen-year-old girl.

Emily   Hello Mum.

A long pause.

They look at each other.

Freya *starts to cry. Horrified. She backs away.*

Emily   Mum –

Freya   I don't ... – Oh god ... you're all *grown up*.
                    Oh god.

Emily *looks upset.*

Freya *pulls herself together and tries to smile.*

Freya   Sorry.

                    Sorry.

                    Your hair.

                    It's a bit like mine.

Emily   I've got dad's nose apparently.

Freya   Yeah.

Emily   His sense of direction too.

They look at each other.

Freya   I look shit to you, probably.

Emily   Well ...

Freya *reaches out and touches her on the arm.*

                 What are you doing?

Freya   Maybe we could, have a coffee. Do you like coffee?

Emily   We don't have time.

Freya   But that's what mums and daughters do. They have a coffee together. They talk. Don't have time before what?

Emily   No, we should go.

Freya *follows* **Emily**.

Jasmine *and* **Colin** *are walking along the river.*

Jasmine   Five.

Colin   Shut up.

Jasmine   Five girls so far, checking you out.

Colin   Right.

Jasmine   How many before today?

Colin   When I was twenty a girl came up to me pinched my bum she obviously thought I looked good from behind but when she turned me round and saw my face she went urrgh, and walked away.

Jasmine   You've had a tough life haven't you?

Colin   Fuck it.

Jasmine   Exactly, you know where we're supposed to be going?

Colin   The South Bank. This way.

*A woman walks past and checks **Colin** out.*

Jasmine   Six.

Colin   !

She chases after him.

Freya *and* **Emily**.

Freya   What are you into?

Emily   What?

Freya   For fun. With your friends.

Emily   I ...

Freya   ?

Emily   Football.

Freya *tries to smile.*

Freya   That's good.

Emily   Mum I –

Freya   Do you have a boyfriend?

Emily   Am I gay you mean?

Freya   No. I just.

Emily   I play football so I must be gay.

Freya   No. I didn't mean that.

Emily   Yeah / okay.

Freya   What do you want to do when you grow up?

Emily   I'll finish school, get a job somewhere probably, I don't know.

Freya	Ambitions . . . ?
Emily	No point is there? I mean there's nowhere to go. You don't understand. Look at you. Thought when you were younger you'd look better.
Freya	What have I done? Why are you being like this?
Emily	Are you joking?
Freya	. . .
Emily	When you've been drinking, you sit on the sofa and apologise again and again. 'I'm sorry, I'm *sorry Emily*'. Then you fall asleep, spill it everywhere. I have to put you to bed.
Freya	What about your dad?
Emily	Dad left ages ago. Only see him Saturdays.
	Come on.
Freya	What?
Emily	We don't want to be late.

Emily *escorts* **Freya** *onwards.*

Steve *is on the South Bank.*

A **Jogger** *jogs past on the way to work.*

Steve	Excuse me.

She comes to a stop.

	I'm . . . meeting someone by the theatre, where's the . . . theatre?
Jogger	The theatre? I don't know.
Steve	Oh, okay –
Jogger	I don't go to the theatre.
Steve	Okay – I just . . .

Jogger   Why would I go to the theatre?

Steve   It doesn't matter.

Jogger   It's just like TV. But more expensive. And further away.

Steve *stops and waits.*

Freya *and* **Emily** *are walking along Waterloo Bridge.*

Emily   You know where they've put the London Eye now?

Freya   No.

Emily   Bath.

Freya   Why?

Emily   Good question. After the flooding it was going to go on tour but no one had the money so they had a public vote and Bath it was instead.

                  You ever been on it? The wheel. I read about Bath in a book once. Looked nice ...

Freya   No.

They stop.

Emily   So what have you done?

Freya   What?

Emily   What do you do? Day to day.

Freya   I ... don't really ... I find it all quite ...

Emily   You find it all too much.

Freya   Yeah.

Emily   You can't cope.

Freya   I've never found it as easy as I think you're supposed to.

Emily *is looking out at the view.*

> Have we stopped then?
>
> Is this where you're taking me?
>
> What am I supposed to do here?

Emily   You've texted Dad haven't you?

Freya   Yes but –

Emily   And Jasmine, and Sarah.

Freya   To meet me. I want to talk to them.

Emily   Look where we're standing. Waterloo Bridge.

Freya   . . .

Emily   You wanted them to watch you. Mum, if you could see what's going to happen. The buildings and the parks are shanty towns. Immigrants everywhere, gambling and drinking, the streets – covered in shit, the air thick with smoke, there's disease and rationing, blackouts and curfews. Every morning when we fetch the water we have to queue for an hour, and at night you keep a knife by the side of your bed, just in case. I hate it. So do you. Everyone has given up. You're passed out on the chair, but I'm in the bed, under the covers, desperately trying to get a message to you. It's what you tell me. It's what you say you should've done, for both of us.

Freya   I'm sorry, I've really been trying.

Emily   It's not too late. Just step over the barrier.

Freya *looks at her.*

Then climbs over the barrier.

>Get used to it. Breathe. I'm sat inside you. Warm and happy and I won't know anything about it. You have my entire support to throw yourself off. It's better you do. I promise.

Freya *looks out.*

>Breathe. And then, imagine there's a step. Just step out. They say most people die of shock before they hit the water.

A few people gather around, at a distance to watch.

Emily *stands amongst them, disappears in the crowd.*

Freya	Emily?
Passer by 1	Who is she?
Passer by 2	I don't know she just climbed over, but look at her.
Passer by 1	Yeah.
Freya	Emily … ?
Passer by 2	Just one of those women.
Passer by 1	/ Yeah, god.
Freya	Emily, please!
Passer by 1	Why does she keep on shouting?
Passer by 2	Who knows? Emily! Fuck! Sorry – shouldn't laugh. Has someone called the police?

Steve *is on the South Bank.*

Jasmine *and* **Colin** *arrive.*

Steve	She texted you too?
Jasmine	Yeah she didn't say you were coming though, could've left you to it.
Steve	Colin, you look –

Colin	Yeah.
Steve	She's supposed to be here supposed to be here by now but –
Jasmine	She gets distracted by bright colours. Don't worry, it's quite normal. She takes her time. Oh no.

Sarah *appears.*

Sarah	Proper family gathering. Steve, she said you were away.
Steve	I was.
Sarah	She's texted everyone. What's happened to you?
Colin	Right.
Jasmine	Colin's got something / to tell you.
Sarah	So where is she?
Steve	I don't know.
Sarah	Drags us all out here then doesn't show up herself, / pretty typical.
Steve	I hoped she'd be waiting here, but –
Sarah	What do you mean Colin's got something / to tell me?
Steve	Has anyone spoken to her? Sorry. / Has anyone actually spoken to Freya?
Sarah	Colin?
Colin	Maybe we should –
Sarah	I didn't take the job. You were right. I turned it down.
Jasmine	He wants a divorce.
Sarah	Oh … you … For fuck's sake Jasmine he buys a new jacket, you think he's having a

	mid life crisis. He doesn't want a divorce, we're just –
Jasmine	Ask him.
Sarah	I'm not going to ask him.
Jasmine	Ask him.
Colin	I think perhaps we should …
Sarah	What? Should what?
Colin	I think perhaps we should.
	Yes.
Steve	Is that …
Jasmine	What?
Sarah	We're, we're not going to talk about it here.
Jasmine	You mean on / the –
Steve	/ Yeah.
Sarah	In front of her and everyone else. We need to –
Colin	Sarah.
Jasmine	/ fuck, fuck, shut up. *Shut up*.
Sarah	I'm not doing this *now*.
Jasmine	On the bridge.

They all look.

A crowd has gathered on the bridge – traffic passes. It is noisy. A **Police Officer** *has arrived.*

Freya	In 1844 Waterloo bridge was called the bridge of sighs, there were so many suicides.
Police Officer	I want you to stay calm.
Freya	Thomas Hood wrote a poem about a homeless woman who threw herself off.

Police Officer   You're going to be alright.

Freya   One more Unfortunate,

Police Officer   Slowly come back/ over the barrier.

Freya   Weary of breath, Rashly importunate,

Police Officer   Help is / on its way.

Freya   Gone to her death.

Passer by 2   / Come on. Fuck's sake, get on with it.

The crowd laughs.

Freya   Make no deep scrutiny
Into her mutiny
Rash and undutiful:

Freya's *phone rings.*

Passer by 2   JUMP JUMP JUMP JUMP ... !

Freya   Fuck fuck shit ...

The crowd chants. **Freya** *answers her phone.*

Steve   Baby, it's me. I'm here. I can see you.

Freya   Steve ... I'm scared. But I can't ... They ...

Freya *cries. Someone in the crowd starts playing 'Jump' by Kris Kross.
The crowd chant.*

Steve   Please. Climb / back down on to the road.

Freya   Who was her mother? /
Had she a sister?

Steve   Calm down, listen. / I'm on my way.

There is a rumbling drowning the rest of the noise. The ground shakes.

An earthquake. The bridge is moving.

Freya   In she plunged boldly –
No matter / how coldly
The rough / river ran –

Steve	Please don't. Freya. / I know what the problem is.
Freya	Cold inhumanity, / Burning insanity,
Steve	Freya. Freya. It's okay. I understand.

The rumbling is loud now. The earth moving.

Freya	Steve. I don't know what to do. I don't want the baby, I really can't have a baby.
Steve	We'll work it out –
Freya	There's a noise. It's moving. Shaking. The bridge. Everything's *moving!*
Steve	Hold on and / just wait or
Freya	I don't want to hold on – I can't wait anymore – It's *too late!* This is important. Where have you *been!* This is *it!*

The earthquake is very loud.

Freya	Oh god oh god, it's the earthquake. Just like they said.
	I can't, I can't do anything.
	Please please no.
	Emily.
	It's breaking.
	I can't hold on! I ... I can't!

She slips.

Blackout.

The sound of destruction.

An earthquake.

End of Act Four.

Act Five

Prologue

As the noise fades, an animation plays.

We see blackboard animation that illustrates the story. The narrator is old and wise.

Narrator   It is said that in the old times, in the early years of the twenty-first century, mankind only thought of himself. The people would steal from the land and plunder the seas, they would kill the animals, tear out the minerals from the ground and poison the sky. And as the earth grew darker, the sun burnt brighter, and the sea began to rise, the people simply closed their eyes and drank, and danced, and attempted to ignore their certain destruction.

It was then, in mankind's greatest hour of need, that Solomon came. A young woman, accompanied only by one faithful companion, packed her bag, and came to the city of London. After three days, walking barefoot, she arrived on the bridge across the river, at the centre of the earth, and she spoke. Her words proclaimed the new enlightenment.

She was young, and so full of hope and truth that her speech, her words, the power and the light, was relayed, repeated, across the world, by radio, by television, by powerful rumour and written instruction to every man and woman on the planet and slowly slowly, the tide turned. People listened and people changed. Solomon spent the rest of her life travelling the world, walking a new path, showing us the future, a new way to live.

And the people of the world were happy. They were saved and they rejoiced.

The blackboard bleaches to white.

Certain Destruction

2525, or possibly a hospital.

A beeping sound.

A clean white space.

Freya *is lying on a single white bed.*

A **Woman** *appears. She looks like* **Grace***, and wears a white version of the floral dress from the Act One Prologue. She also wears a veil.*

Grace	Freya.
	Freya?

Freya *wakes. Tries to sit up.*

	No, you don't need to move.
Freya	I was in the river.
Grace	You're safe now.
Freya	These aren't my clothes ...
Grace	How do you feel?
Freya	Where am I? Where is everyone?
Grace	It's just me. Try to focus. You've been asleep a very long time.
Freya	What do you mean?
Grace	You're in the future.
Freya	The future?
Grace	The year Twenty Five, Twenty Five.
Freya	You're joking.
Grace	You're alive. You're warm. You're safe. And now you're awake.

Have a drink.
Here.
A glass of water.

Freya *takes it, and drinks.*

Freya   Who are you?

Grace   I'm Grace.

Freya   My mum was called Grace.

Grace   Yes.

Freya   But she died. There was nothing they could do. It was cancer.

Grace   We don't have cancer any more.

Freya   Good.

Grace   We don't have diseases or pain, we don't have suffering or death, we have only peace. Peace and life.

Grace *strokes* **Freya**'*s hair.*

Freya   She used to stroke my head like that.

Can I …

Freya *removes* **Grace**'*s veil.*

Mum …

Grace   Hello Freya.

Freya   Mum!

I was so scared! I didn't … I didn't know what to do.

Freya *hugs her and cries.* **Grace** *hugs her tight.*

Grace   You're safe.
You're safe now.

Hospital

Freya *is in a hospital bed, on a ventilator, unconscious.*

Steve *is watching her.*

He paces.

Tim *enters.*

Tim	Mr Sullivan?
Steve	Yes?
Tim	I was the doctor who treated your wife. They said you had some questions.
Steve	When she came in, didn't you think there was something wrong?
Tim	She was worried about the baby but we tried to put her mind at rest, we let her stay in overnight, and then in the morning she checked herself out. We had no reason to think she would ... well.
Steve	You just let her go.
Tim	It was out assessment that she would be fine.
Steve	Just let her walk out the door by herself.
Tim	She said she didn't have anyone to collect her.

They look at each other.

Steve	What do you think?
Tim	I'm sorry –
Steve	Does she have a chance?
Tim	I'm sorry, it's not my department.
Steve	I'm sure you've spoken to your colleagues before coming in here, you all *talk*, don't you? You wanted to know the situation before you confronted the husband. So you know the situation, what do you think?

Tim	They're conducting some tests.
Steve	But what do you think?
Tim	
Steve	If there isn't a chance, you should tell me. If there's nothing any of us can do anymore and we should all just give up, I'd rather know.
Tim	I'm sure there's a chance.
Steve	
Tim	You might want to talk to her.
Steve	Why? She's in a coma. Why would I talk to her?
Tim	Some people find it helpful.
Steve	...
Tim	Is there anything else I can do?
Steve	Her family are outside. Can you ... make sure they have what they want, tell them what's going on, get them whatever they need.
	And keep them out.
	I don't want them coming in here.

Tim *goes.*

2525

The music plays again. **Grace** *enters.*

Freya *is sat on the edge of the bed.*

Freya	So – Dad bought into one of those cryogenic things and we've all been frozen at the point of death, you as well, revitalised only when medical science has the power to heal us.

Grace *smiles.*

> Is that right?

Grace *just looks at her.*

> Is that what's going on?

Grace   You look better.

Freya   I feel better. I want to have a look round. The future! Have you got flying cars?

Grace   We don't need cars.

Freya   And robots.

Grace   You have no idea.

Freya   When can I see?

Grace   When you're well enough.

Freya   I'm fine, look.

Grace   We have some questions first.

Freya   What about?

Grace   Freya, the date of your preservation is of vital historical significance. It is said, that this was the turning point. The moment you fell, the place it happened, Legend has it that it was from that place at that time that the speech was made. From the bridge. From that moment. The tide turned. The world became better, and better until we solved the problems. All the problems. And we survived.

> So. Did you hear it? Did you hear the speech? Is that why you were there?

Freya   No. I don't know anything about it.

Grace   This is important, you were on the bridge, in that time.

Freya	Yes but –
Grace	Why were you on the bridge, if not to hear the Solomon's speech?
Freya	Solomon?
Grace	Yes.
Freya	Solomon on the bridge?
Grace	Solomon, the greatest woman in the world, she walked to London, stood at the centre of the earth and changed everything.
Freya	Solomon ... Mum. It's not Solomon. It's Sullivan.
Grace	What?
Freya	It's me. I walked all the way to the bridge, I stood in the centre of the earth.
Grace	But Freya ...
Freya	I'm Solomon. I changed the world.
Grace	Freya you can't be.
Freya	Yes! Why not?
Grace	Because you died. And Solomon ... Solomon lived.

Sarah *and* **Colin** *are in the hospital café.* **Sarah** *brings back two coffees.*

Sarah	There.
Colin	Thanks.

They drink.

Colin	How are you?

Sarah *shrugs.*

They drink.

Sarah	Do you remember the jacket you wore at Suzie's party?
Colin	What?
Sarah	I just thought of it. You remember? It had shoulder pads.
Colin	Yes.
Sarah	It was far too big.
Colin	My lucky jacket.
Sarah	Well, that's what you used to call it –
Colin	Yeah.
Sarah	Lucky in what way exactly?
Colin	It got attention.
Sarah	You looked stupid.
Colin	Like I said, attention.
Sarah	Well …
Colin	From the birds.
Sarah	Birds. Jesus.
Colin	Got your attention.
Sarah	You used to roll up the sleeves.
Colin	Nothing wrong with that, not in the eighties.

He rolls up the sleeves of his jacket.

See?

She smiles.

Good look.

He unrolls them.

Sarah   Probably just ruined it.

Colin   What?

Sarah   That jacket.

Colin   What do you mean?

Sarah   Just ... that it ... looks expensive, you probably shouldn't –

Colin   Not your problem now is it?

Sarah   Colin ...

Colin   What?

Sarah   I was trying to –

Colin   What?

Sarah

Colin   We shouldn't talk about this now.

Sarah   When you lost your job yes I probably thought I should compensate in some way. I know things aren't like they were, I know I'm *different* these days. But I don't think it's too late.

I'll change.

Or something.

Colin   Do you like this suit?

Sarah   Yeah, I mean ...

Colin   Honestly.

Sarah   ...

I don't think it's very ... It's not who you are.

Colin   I love it. I really do.
It is absolutely, who I am.
It absolutely is.

Sarah   ...

Sarah *reaches to him.*

He moves away.

Sarah   Do you even like me?
                 I mean.
                 You say you've fallen out of love with me
                 and
                 that's ... fine ... that's ...
                 You don't want to see me any more.

Colin

Sarah   But do you think I'm a nice person?
                 Because, with what everyone's said.
                 With Freya.
                 And what Jasmine says.

                 I don't have anyone else.

                 So this is kind of crucial.

                 Colin?

                 Do you like me?

Colin   You live in a million pound house with two
                 cars. You're a Liberal Democrat minister in a
                 Tory government. Then you tell me you
                 want to join the board of a multinational
                 airline. It's not that I don't like you Sarah. I
                 hardly know you.

                 Jasmine was right.

Sarah   Jasmine's never been right about anything.

Colin   ...

Sarah   What did she say?

Colin   Things change.

They look at each other.

2525. **Freya** *is on her feet now.*

Freya	Then ... then I have to go back and do what I was supposed to do.
Grace	Back? Freya you can't go back. That world crumbled to dust hundreds of years ago. This is all that exists now.
Freya	But I was supposed to say something. That's why Peter was there. And Emily. I wasn't supposed to fall, I was supposed to speak. The crowd was there, ready to listen, I was supposed to give them the message.
Grace	Freya come and sit down.
Freya	But I messed it up. There must be something you can do.
Grace	It's too late.
Freya	Mum!
Grace	Sit down!
Freya	No. I'm getting out. I've got to find someone who can help.
	I ...
	Oh.
	Where's the door? There isn't a door.
Grace	No.
Freya	How do you get in and out?
Grace	Freya.
Freya	What?
Grace	You don't need to go anywhere. Everything's good here. Everything's perfect.
Freya	And where is everyone? You keep on saying we think this, and we're very interested, but

I've only seen you. There should be hundreds of people wanting to talk to me, I'm historically important remember.

Grace   I'm your closest relative and carer, of course I'm the one to look after you and if you give it time you'll –

Freya   There's something going on.

Grace   . . .

Freya   Please. Mum. Don't lie to me.

Grace looks at her.

I always knew when something was wrong.

Grace   Have you got a headache?

Freya   How did you know?

Grace   Sit down, with me, on the bed, and I'll explain.

Jasmine is in the waiting room.

Robert enters.

Jasmine   Er. This is a private room?

Robert   Really?

Jasmine   We've paid for it.

Robert   I'm sure you have.

Jasmine   Family only yeah?

She looks at him properly.

Oh. Shit. Shit.

Shit, didn't recognise you. Jesus. Seen pictures but they must be from a while back. You look ... old. Shame we haven't met before something like this, isn't it?

Robert	You look . . . really –
Jasmine	What? Here you go, they said you like to answer back, okay yeah, I've been up all night, I'm not my best. What? I look like what?
Robert	Like your mother.
Jasmine	Do I?
Robert	When she was your age.

She's floored.

Jasmine	Yeah right well done. Good tactic. I look like my mum, put me off my – That must freak you out then. Sarah says Mum was never happy, often crying she said, looks like Freya got those genes.
Robert	Look, I know there's a lot to talk / about but –
Jasmine	And I got yours, apparently I've got a mouth on me reminds Sarah of you, yeah there's a fuck of a lot to talk about where do you want to start?
Robert	This isn't the time.
Jasmine	Never is, is it? Never is the fucking time by the sound of it.
Robert	Jasmine –
Jasmine	Such a lonely old fucking – look at you –
Robert	You're not a teenager so –
Jasmine	Actually I am.
Robert	Can you stop –
Jasmine	Technically I am? Nineteen, if you're counting, which you're probably not, so – stop what?

Robert	Stop being so fucking petulant.
Jasmine	Christ they said you got nasty quickly I thought they meant hours not minutes look at you, big red face.
Robert	Sit down.
Jasmine	I'm not the one getting angry Gandalf, you're shouting, I don't think you're allowed to do that I might call security.
Robert	I hate planes. I'm shattered. Fine. You're nineteen. I'm seventy. Sit down, and shut up. What are you wearing?
Jasmine	Whatever the fuck I want.
Robert	You look like prostitute.
Jasmine	You talk like this to everyone?
Robert	Yes. You?
Jasmine	Yes.

A moment of respect.

Robert	Good.

He sits.

She reluctantly sits as well.

Jasmine	Read your books.
Robert	And?
Jasmine	Bit dry.

He smiles.

	You told her to get rid of it.
Robert	I told her the truth yes.
Jasmine	Probably regret that now.

A moment.

Robert   I could do with a drink.

Jasmine *takes a bottle out of her bag. Gives it to* **Robert**.

                 What's this?

Jasmine   Ouzo.

Robert   Oh.

He drinks from the bottle. It's awful.

                 You want some?

She takes the bottle. Drinks. They continue to share it.

Robert   I should've put my work first, from the
                 beginning. That's what I regret.

Jasmine   Even though Freya's nearly dead.
                 Sarah's a fuck up, getting divorced.
                 And me ... well ... look.
                 Even given all that?

Robert   Because of all that exactly.

                 I should never have had any of you in the
                 first place.

Jasmine   So why have you come now?

Robert   To say goodbye.

Jasmine   She's not –

Robert   Yes. From what I understand she doesn't
                 have much of a chance.

Jasmine   No fuck off you don't know if anything had
                 happened Steve would've told us, you don't
                 know shit. Fuck's sake. Thought you'd have
                 big eyes actually. We've all got big eyes.
                 Suppose it must've been Mum.

Robert   Yes.

Jasmine	Right.
Robert	But she had your hair. Your hands.
Jasmine	What else?
Robert	...
Jasmine	What's in the bag?
Robert	One of your mother's dresses. Freya liked it, wanted it, years ago. I wouldn't let her. I thought maybe I could ...
Jasmine	Bit fucking late now.
Robert	You're not like the other two.
Jasmine	No. You would've liked me.
Robert	Yes.
	I think I would.

Sarah *enters*

Sarah	You're here.
Robert	I am.
Sarah	You've met.
Robert	We have.
Jasmine	Where's Colin?
Sarah	Colin's gone.

As the next scene continues, **Sarah** *sits with them and drinks the Ouzo.*

2525.

Grace	When you fell in the river, Freya, you hit your head. You did some damage. And sometimes, when that happens, people become unable to see a distinction between their own particles and those around them. They can't see the edges of their body

anymore – where they stop and the world begins. They can instead understand instinctively that we are all just different recycled pieces of a larger, older creature. We are simply earthquakes ourselves, wonderful irregularities in an evolving system. We die and the earth uses us for something new.

Young **Robert** *enters, dressed in white, and wheels in a cot.*

Yes Freya, this is the future, and I am your mother. But this is also the past and the present, and I am your father, your sisters, your friends, your husband, the table, the bed, the ground, we are everyone that is, was, and everything that will be. I'm nature all in one. So are you.

Freya   This isn't real.

Grace   Your brain is doing what it always does. Making sense of what it receives. Combining imagination, memory, information.

Freya   I'm dreaming.

Grace   You're on your way.

Freya   Where?

Grace   We're here to help you.

Young Robert   Freya. Look.

The sound of a baby crying. **Freya** *goes and looks in the cot. She picks up the baby.*

Freya   Emily.

Doctor Harris *is with* **Steve***, who sits on the bed.*

Doctor Harris   I'm sorry. Her condition is worsening.

Steve   I . . .

Steve *doesn't know how to react.*

Doctor Harris It's a matter of when to say goodbye. It should be soon.

Steve Alright. Yes.

Doctor Harris Alright then.

And what about the family? I know they're outside.

Steve . . .

Doctor Harris Will they want to be here?

Steve

Doctor Harris Or would you rather it was just you?

Steve Let them in.

The family goes through.

The **Nurse** *sits in a chair, exhausted. Turns on the radio. Music plays.*

A hymn.

2525

The worlds beginning to merge.

Freya *frantic.*

Freya Wake me up . . . please.

Grace No.

Freya Please. I need to go back. I can't stay here. Emily's alive. I can hear her. She's calling for me.

Grace Freya. You can't.

Freya I made a mistake. I need to go back.

Tell them all. Give the speech. Walk the earth.

Grace	No.
Freya	You can't stop me. This isn't real. I need to wake up and tell them what's going to happen, or the world doesn't change. The world stays as it is!
	Darling!

*She puts **Emily** back in the cot.*

> I'm going to be with you. I'm going to wake up.

Freya *goes to the bed, lies down and shuts her eyes.*

Grace	Freya. I'm sorry.
Freya	Now!
	Yes!
	Now!
Grace	It's over.

*The music continues, the worlds blurring. The family gathered around the bed, **Grace** stood slightly apart.*

We can't hear what's happening – the music plays.

Doctor Harris *stands close by.* **Steve** *sits on the bed with* **Freya**, *holding* **Emily**.

One by one the family say goodbye. **Robert** *stands back and watches.*

Steve *gives* **Emily** *to* **Sarah**, *and then lifts* **Freya** *and hugs her. Crying.*

Some distance away ... during this, **Emily** *enters, sixteen, very different to how we saw her before. Bright, optimistic, intelligent.*

She wears the floral dress worn by **Grace** *in the Part One prologue. And she carries a back pack.*

Epilogue

The kitchen of a large house in the west Oxfordshire countryside. Night. On the table there is food out.

It is sixteen years later.

Emily *is packing food into a backpack.*

Some of it doesn't fit. In the rearranging, we see a map, a torch.

A knock on the door.

Emily *goes and opens it.*

Tom *enters, now thirty-five, a man, rather than a boy. He is dressed much better, ready for a long walk. He is sure of himself.*

Emily	Shhh – / Dad's asleep – you look nervous.
Tom	You've barely left the town on your own before, you don't know what it's like.
Emily	I've done my research.
Tom	You should let me come with you.

She smiles. Touches his arm.

Emily	I'll be fine.
Tom	And what are you wearing?
Emily	Do you like it? Before she died, Mum told Dad it was her favourite dress. Dad gave it to me this afternoon, for my birthday. I like the pattern. How about you? Did you get me a present?

Tom *gives her a small bag.*

Tom	Papers, ID, map, new phone.
Emily	Good.
Tom	All in the bag, as ordered.
Emily	Perfect. I'm thinking maybe I should go barefoot...

Tom   It's a long way.

Emily   It is, and people should notice.

She takes her shoes off.

Definitely barefoot.

Tom   You'll call me if you get into trouble?

Emily   There won't be trouble.

Tom   There might be, maybe we should tell your dad what you're doing. If he wakes up and you're gone –

Emily   When did you care what he thought?

Tom   This is different.

Emily   I've told them for years, over and over, when I'm sixteen, this is what happens. At dawn, I'll be on my way. Not my fault if they never believed me.

Tom   At least leave a note –

Emily   Right. Toothbrush, bag, towel.

She puts the backpack on.

Tom   Speech?

Emily   Don't need a speech. It's all up here ... Tom! I'm half your age and you look petrified.

Tom   It's ridiculous.

Emily   You know what I can do?

Tom   Yes.

Emily   And you trust me?

Tom   Of course.

Emily   Then smile. It'll be fine. Now, how do I look?

He looks at her, takes her in.

Tom   Emily Sullivan.

Magnificent.

She smiles.

He smiles too.

She looks at him, goes to the kitchen blackboard, and writes, in large letters.

'Gone to London'

As she goes on her way, **Steve** *finally lets go of* **Freya***, and she dies.*

Blackout.

End of Play.

Headlong

Headlong makes exhilarating, provocative and spectacular
new work to take around the country and around the world.

'*The country's most
exciting touring company*'
Daily Telegraph

'*Wild, mad and deeply
intelligent theatre*'
Sunday Times

Led by award-winning Artistic Director
Rupert Goold, Headlong is one of the UK's
leading theatre companies. *Earthquakes
in London* was commissioned by Headlong
in 2008 and developed as part of our
ongoing commitment to new work. We
collaborate with the most exciting and
adventurous theatre artists in the country
and provide them with the time, resources
and creative support to allow them to
make their most challenging work.

Headlong Theatre is:

Rupert Goold	Artistic Director
Henny Finch	Executive Producer
Jenni Kershaw	Executive Producer (Maternity Cover)
Robert Icke	Associate Director
Julie Renwick	Finance Manager
Lindsey Alvis	Assistant Producer
Louisa Norman	Assistant Producer
Jamie Lloyd	Associate Artist

Photo credit: Tristram Kenton
Original cast photo

www.headlongtheatre.co.uk

Methuen Drama Modern Plays

include work by

Edward Albee
Jean Anouilh
John Arden
Margaretta D'Arcy
Peter Barnes
Sebastian Barry
Brendan Behan
Dermot Bolger
Edward Bond
Bertolt Brecht
Howard Brenton
Anthony Burgess
Simon Burke
Jim Cartwright
Caryl Churchill
Complicite
Noël Coward
Lucinda Coxon
Sarah Daniels
Nick Darke
Nick Dear
Shelagh Delaney
David Edgar
David Eldridge
Dario Fo
Michael Frayn
John Godber
Paul Godfrey
David Greig
John Guare
Peter Handke
David Harrower
Jonathan Harvey
Iain Heggie
Declan Hughes
Terry Johnson
Sarah Kane
Charlotte Keatley
Barrie Keeffe

Howard Korder
Robert Lepage
Doug Lucie
Martin McDonagh
John McGrath
Terrence McNally
David Mamet
Patrick Marber
Arthur Miller
Mtwa, Ngema & Simon
Tom Murphy
Phyllis Nagy
Peter Nichols
Sean O'Brien
Joseph O'Connor
Joe Orton
Louise Page
Joe Penhall
Luigi Pirandello
Stephen Poliakoff
Franca Rame
Mark Ravenhill
Philip Ridley
Reginald Rose
Willy Russell
Jean-Paul Sartre
Sam Shepard
Wole Soyinka
Simon Stephens
Shelagh Stephenson
Peter Straughan
C. P. Taylor
Theatre Workshop
Sue Townsend
Judy Upton
Timberlake Wertenbaker
Roy Williams
Snoo Wilson
Victoria Wood

Methuen Drama Student Editions

Jean Anouilh *Antigone* • John Arden *Serjeant Musgrave's Dance*
Alan Ayckbourn *Confusions* • Aphra Behn *The Rover* • Edward Bond
Lear • *Saved* • Bertolt Brecht *The Caucasian Chalk Circle* • *Fear and
Misery in the Third Reich* • *The Good Person of Szechwan* • *Life of Galileo* •
Mother Courage and her Children • *The Resistible Rise of Arturo Ui* • *The
Threepenny Opera* • Anton Chekhov *The Cherry Orchard* • *The Seagull* •
Three Sisters • *Uncle Vanya* • Caryl Churchill *Serious Money* • *Top Girls*
• Shelagh Delaney *A Taste of Honey* • Euripides *Elektra* • *Medea* •
Dario Fo *Accidental Death of an Anarchist* • Michael Frayn *Copenhagen*
• John Galsworthy *Strife* • Nikolai Gogol *The Government Inspector* •
Robert Holman *Across Oka* • Henrik Ibsen *A Doll's House* • *Ghosts* •
Hedda Gabler • Charlotte Keatley *My Mother Said I Never Should* •
Bernard Kops *Dreams of Anne Frank* • Federico García Lorca *Blood
Wedding* • *Doña Rosita the Spinster* (bilingual edition) • *The House of
Bernarda Alba* • (bilingual edition) • *Yerma* (bilingual edition) • David
Mamet *Glengarry Glen Ross* • *Oleanna* • Patrick Marber *Closer* • John
Marston *Malcontent* • Martin McDonagh *The Lieutenant of Inishmore* •
Joe Orton *Loot* • Luigi Pirandello *Six Characters in Search of an Author*
• Mark Ravenhill *Shopping and F***ing* • Willy Russell *Blood Brothers*
• *Educating Rita* • Sophocles *Antigone* • *Oedipus the King* • Wole
Soyinka *Death and the King's Horseman* • Shelagh Stephenson *The
Memory of Water* • August Strindberg *Miss Julie* • J. M. Synge *The
Playboy of the Western World* • Theatre Workshop *Oh What a Lovely
War* Timberlake Wertenbaker *Our Country's Good* • Arnold Wesker
The Merchant • Oscar Wilde *The Importance of Being Earnest* •
Tennessee Williams *A Streetcar Named Desire* • *The Glass Menagerie*

Methuen Drama Modern Classics

Jean Anouilh *Antigone* • Brendan Behan *The Hostage* • Robert Bolt *A Man for All Seasons* • Edward Bond *Saved* • Bertolt Brecht *The Caucasian Chalk Circle* • *Fear and Misery in the Third Reich* • *The Good Person of Szechwan* • *Life of Galileo* • *The Messingkauf Dialogues* • *Mother Courage and Her Children* • *Mr Puntila and His Man Matti* • *The Resistible Rise of Arturo Ui* • *Rise and Fall of the City of Mahagonny* • *The Threepenny Opera* • Jim Cartwright *Road* • *Two & Bed* • Caryl Churchill *Serious Money* • *Top Girls* • Noël Coward *Blithe Spirit* • *Hay Fever* • *Present Laughter* • *Private Lives* • *The Vortex* • Shelagh Delaney *A Taste of Honey* • Dario Fo *Accidental Death of an Anarchist* • Michael Frayn *Copenhagen* • Lorraine Hansberry *A Raisin in the Sun* • Jonathan Harvey *Beautiful Thing* • David Mamet *Glengarry Glen Ross* • *Oleanna* • *Speed-the-Plow* • Patrick Marber *Closer* • *Dealer's Choice* • Arthur Miller *Broken Glass* • Percy Mtwa, Mbongeni Ngema, Barney Simon *Woza Albert!* • Joe Orton *Entertaining Mr Sloane* • *Loot* • *What the Butler Saw* • Mark Ravenhill *Shopping and F***ing* • Willy Russell *Blood Brothers* • *Educating Rita* • *Stags and Hens* • *Our Day Out* • Jean-Paul Sartre *Crime Passionnel* • Wole Soyinka • *Death and the King's Horseman* • Theatre Workshop *Oh, What a Lovely War* • Frank Wedekind • *Spring Awakening* • Timberlake Wertenbaker *Our Country's Good*

Methuen Drama World Classics

include

Jean Anouilh (two volumes)
Brendan Behan
Aphra Behn
Bertolt Brecht (eight volumes)
Büchner
Bulgakov
Calderón
Čapek
Anton Chekhov
Noël Coward (eight volumes)
Feydeau (two volumes)
Eduardo De Filippo
Max Frisch
John Galsworthy
Gogol
Gorky (two volumes)
Harley Granville Barker
  (two volumes)
Victor Hugo
Henrik Ibsen (six volumes)
Jarry

Lorca (three volumes)
Marivaux
Mustapha Matura
David Mercer (two volumes)
Arthur Miller (six volumes)
Molière
Musset
Peter Nichols (two volumes)
Joe Orton
A. W. Pinero
Luigi Pirandello
Terence Rattigan
  (two volumes)
W. Somerset Maugham
  (two volumes)
August Strindberg
  (three volumes)
J. M. Synge
Ramón del Valle-Inclán
Frank Wedekind
Oscar Wilde